PENGUIN BOOKS

MOTHERLAND FATHERLAND HOMELANDSEXUALS

'[Lockwood] has written a book at once angrier, and more fun, more attuned to our time and more bizarre, than most poetry can ever get, a book easy to recommend for people who do not read new poetry often – as well as for people who do'

Stephen Burt, *The New York Times Sunday Book Review*

'Lockwood's "Rape Joke" is . . . one of the most amazing poems I've read recently . . . [S]he delights in the absurdity of her materials, turning the spectacle up to 11 while she lets its component parts slip loose . . . She loves to personify the inhuman at the same time as she depersonalizes the human, creating a swirl of slippery images out of our already ridiculous conceptions . . . The poems go further, . . . letting the absurd implications of American life and language turn unreal and real, divorce and marry or, more often, simply get it on . . . For the nimble, the skeptical, and the restless, writing like this represents a way to *be* in a country whose failures seem to them as much aesthetic as they are ethical . . . Lockwood's poems are less a critique of that culture than an alternative opened up sideways to it, a place made of the mind's freedom to move through it on its own outrageous, occasionally indifferent, improvisatory terms'

Jonathan Farmer, *Slate*

'The little hairs on my back rose often while reading *Motherland Fatherland Homelandsexuals* . . . That's biological praise, the most fundamental kind, impossible to fake'

Dwight Garner, *The New York Times*

WITHDRAWN

Patricia Lockwood was born in Fort Wayne, Indiana, USA and raised in all the worst cities of the Midwest. Her debut collection, *Balloon Pop Outlaw Black*, was released in 2012 by Octopus Books; a selection of her poetry was included in *Penguin Modern Poets 2: Controlled Explosions* (2016), and her memoir, *Priestdaddy*, was published by Penguin in 2017. Her poems have appeared widely, including in *The New Yorker*, the *London Review of Books*, *Tin House* and *Poetry*.

PATRICIA LOCKWOOD

Motherland
Fatherland
Homelandsexuals

PENGUIN BOOKS

PENGUIN BOOKS

UK | USA | Canada | Ireland | Australia
India | New Zealand | South Africa

Penguin Books is part of the Penguin Random House group of companies
whose addresses can be found at global.penguinrandomhouse.com.

First published in the United States of America by Penguin Books 2014
First published in Great Britain in Penguin Books 2017

001

Typeset in 10/13.75 pt Warnock Pro by Jouve (UK), Milton Keynes
Printed in Great Britain by Clays Ltd, St Ives plc

A CIP catalogue record for this book is available from the British Library

ISBN: 978-0-141-98486-5

www.greenpenguin.co.uk

Penguin Random House is committed to a
sustainable future for our business, our readers
and our planet. This book is made from Forest
Stewardship Council® certified paper.

CONTENTS

Is Your Country a He or a She in Your Mouth

Mine is a man I think, I love men, they call me
a fatherlandsexual, all the motherlandsexuals
have been sailed away, and there were never
any here in the first place, they tell us. Myself
I have never seen a mountain, myself I have
never seen a valley, especially not my own,
I am afraid of the people who live there,
who eat hawk and wild rice from my pelvic
bone. Oh no, I am fourteen, I have walked
into my motherland's bedroom, her body
is indistinguishable from the fatherland
who is 'loving her' from behind, so close
their borders match up, except for a notable
Area belonging to the fatherland. I am drawn
to the motherland's lurid sunsets, I am reaching
my fingers to warm them, the people in my
valley are scooping hawk like crazy, I can no
longer tell which country is which, salt air off
both their coasts, so gross, where is a good nice gulp
of Midwestern pre-tornado? The tornado above me
has sucked up a Cow, the motherland declares,
the tornado above him has sucked up a Bull,
she says pointing to the fatherland. But the cow
is clearly a single cow, chewing a single cud
of country, chewing their countries into one,
and 'I hate these country!' I scream, and
their eyes shine with rain and fog, because
at last I am using the accent of the homeland,
at last I am a homelandsexual and I will never
go away from them, there will one day be two
of you too they say, but I am boarding myself
already, I recede from their coasts like a Superferry

packed stem to stern with citizens, all waving hellos
and goodbyes, and at night all my people go below
and gorge themselves with hunks of hawk,
      the traditional dish of the new floating heartland.

Search 'Lizard Vagina' and You Shall Find

A higher country had a question, a higher
country searched and found me, and the name
        of the country was north of me, Canada.
When I think of you I think *up there* just as I
        think when I think of my brain, my brain
and the bad sunning lizard inside it. Today
you searched 'lizard vagina', Canada. It is so
hugely small if you can imagine it; it is scaled
it is scaled so far down. It evolved over many
millions of years to be perfectly invisible to you;
and so you will never see it, Canada. Here is
some pornography, if it will help: tongues flick
out all over the desert! Next time try *thunder*
lizard vagina. That will be big enough for even
        you, Canada. You have one somewhere
in your hills, or else somewhere in your badlands.
Perhaps someone is uncovering a real one right
now, with a pickaxe a passion and a patience.
Ever since she was a child she knew what she
would do. She buttons her background-colored
clothes, she bends down to her work;
                        keep spreading,
        Canada, she will show you to yourself.
Your *down there* that is, my Up There. Oh South oh
South oh South you think, oh West oh West now West
say you. The pickaxe the passion and the patience
        hears, pink tongue between her lips just thinking.
The stones and the sand and the hollows they watch
        her. The tip of her tongue thinks almost out loud,
'I have a brain am in a brain brain suns itself in lizard
        too. Where would I be if I were what I wanted?'
Has a feeling finally, swings the pickaxe- the passion-
                and the patience-tip down.

| 3

The Whole World Gets Together and Gangbangs a Deer

Bambi is fresh from the countryside. Bambi is fresh
and we want him on film. He doesn't even know
how to kiss yet. 'Lean in and part your lips,' we say,
'and pull a slow strip off a tree.' We shine our biggest
spotlight on him, our biggest spotlight is the sun.
And under the spotlight the deer drips sweat, and what
do deer like more than salt. 'Now look at the fawn
and grow an antler,' we patiently instruct him. 'It will
grow from your thoughts like the ones on your head.'
Oh Bambi says the fawn, oh Bambi. Fresh grass-stains
around the young mouth. Every deer gets called Bambi
at least once in its life, every deer must answer to Bambi,
every deer hears don't kill Bambi, every deer hears don't
eat Bambi, every deer hears LOOK OH LOOK it's Bambi.
When the deer all die they will die of genericide, of one
baby name for the million of them. Then women begin
to be called Bambi, and then deer understand what women
are like: light-shafts of long blond hair and long legs.
The sun piercing through the Bavarian trees and the sun
touching down on the dewy green ground. Then women
begin to be called Fawn, and then women begin to say
Bambi oh Bambi. And their mouths are open and they
gape like a mouth when it takes a big bite of spring green.
The spotlight shines down through the trees in long legs.

This is the first movie most of us see. Small name
for a small deer: Bambi. Sometimes he feels *all* the deer
could fit inside him. The movie we are making is this one:

all the deer in one deer one after another. Subtitles
so we know what his soft sounds are saying. Mostly he says
THE MEADOW, THE MEADOW! like the women who are
Bambi say GOD OH GOD. What they mean is a wide open

space, a great clearing. All the deer and us watching in a great
open field. A great wide clearing in the face of the deer
says THE MEADOW, THE MEADOW! and all of us watching.
The deer's mouths moving as if they are reading.

But no, they are eating the grass.

He Marries the Stuffed-Owl Exhibit
at the Indiana Welcome Center

He marries her mites and the wires in her wings,
he marries her yellow glass eyes and black centers,
he marries her near-total head turn, he marries
        the curve of each of her claws, he marries
the information plaque, he marries the extinction
        of this kind of owl, he marries the owl
that she loved in life and the last thought of him
in the thick of her mind
        just one inch away from the bullet, there,
                he marries the moths
who make holes in the owl, who have eaten the owl
almost all away, he marries the branch of the tree
that she grips, he marries the real-looking moss
and dead leaves, he marries the smell of must
that surrounds her, he marries the strong blue
        stares of children, he marries nasty smudges
of their noses on the glass, he marries the camera
that points at the owl to make sure no one steals her,
so the camera won't object when he breaks the glass
while reciting some vows that he wrote himself,
he screams OWL instead of I'LL and then ALWAYS
LOVE HER, he screams HAVE AND TO HOLD
and takes hold of the owl and wrenches the owl
away from her branch
        and he covers her in kisses and the owl
thinks, 'More moths,' and at the final hungry kiss,
'That must have been the last big bite, there is no more
of me left to eat and thank God,' when he marries
the stuffing out of the owl and hoots as the owl flies out
under his arm, they elope into the darkness of Indiana,
Indiana he screams is their new life and WELCOME.

They live in a tree together now, and the children of
Welcome to Indiana say who even more than usual,
and the children of Welcome to Indiana they wonder
where they belong. Not in Indiana, they say to themselves,
the state of all-consuming love, we cannot belong in Indiana,
      as night falls and the moths appear one by one, hungry.

An Animorph Enters the Doggie-Dog World

Discover the power at age eleven. Discover all powers
at age eleven. A kittenhead struggles out of your face
and the kittenhead mews MILK, you gasp with its
mouth and it slurps itself back. Yet the mew for MILK
remains, you drink it. You think, 'I am an Animorph.'
Your sight and your hearing increase, like wheat
and the wind in the wheat. Well you've never seen
any wheat but it sounds good, to you and your new
trembling ears. Blue sky increases above the wheat
and you know what it's like to grow a . . . well.
A hawk's is between two legs but much higher.

Halfway to any animal is where you like
to be. Get halfway there and have just the instinct,
the instinct that someone's approaching. Stripes

begin to form, are always a surprise, you look
down and you move your head left to right and then
the meaning comes. English get worse but not much
in your muzzle, English get worse but not much
in your mouth. You walk to school and sit next
to a girl who was born with a tail and you copy off
her. You rub your temples when they ache, rub any
of your body when it aches, you seem to be only
a series of places where animal parts could emerge.
Soon you will be a teenager, and soon you will be
so greasy, and how you can hardly wait, because:
its grease makes the animal graceful, and go. You go
to the petting zoo with your class and timidly reach

in a hand. Turn to a donkey and finally
feel your lashes are long enough. Turn to a horse
and finally feel that your eyes are so meltingly human.
Walk home on your own through the fields and the fields,
and the increase of wheat and the wind in it, and think

of the life that stretches before you: work your way
through all the animals, and come to the end of them,
and what? And turn to crickets, and make no noise?
One tear struggles out of your face, but no that's not
a tear. 'I fuckin eat crickets,' your kittenhead says,
'I fuckin eat silence of crickets for fun. I got life after
life and a name like Baby. Every time I try to cry a tear
a new kittenhead grows out of me.' And oh how you
are lifted, then,

        the kittenhead of you in the high hawk hold.

The Hatfields and McCoys

I am waiting for the day when the Hatfields
and McCoys finally become interesting to me,
when they flare with significance at last as if
they'd been written in Early Times Whiskey
and the match of my sight had been flicked
and was racing now along them, and racing

      like a line to their houses – who wasted
all this whiskey, and now everything is lit up:
how they hid behind trunks of oaks, and hid
behind herds of cows, how they aimed like teats
at each other and shot death in a straight white
line; I will learn how it began, probably over
a . . . *gal*, or McCoy gave a Hatfield an unfair
grade for a paper about mammals he worked
really hard on, and his dad to whom grades
were life and death kindled a torch in the night,
and burned her grading hand to ashes along
with all the rest of her, but her name McCoy
escaped from the fire and woke up in seven

      brothers. I will learn how
their underdrawers fought each other while
hanging on the line, how socks disappeared
from their pairs, how new mailmen were killed
every day touching poisoned postcards they sent
to each other, which said things like Wish you
WERENT here, and *GOODBYE* from sunny Spain,
I will learn precise numbers of people who died
and where they put all the bodies, under the garden
maybe, where they helped grow blood-red carrots
that longed to lodge in enemy throats,

      where they helped grow brooding tomatoes
that were still considered deadly back then, as part

of the nightshade family. Two of their babies
fell in love, because love comes earlier for people
        who live in the past and the mountains,
            and when they turned one year old
they were told they were Hatfields and McCoys,
and one locked his lips grimly on a breast that night
and drank milk until he died, the other took an entire
bottle of Doctor Samson's Soothing Syrup for Crybaby
Boys, two-hundred-proof I read somewhere, and his throat went
whoosh and he died too. Who was the final McCoy
or Hatfield? He says point a gun at me, then maybe

        I'll know where I am. What else, I will learn
what year it was, and lift my head from reading
a full year later, finished with Hatfields and McCoys,
my sight on fire will have gutted their houses, the line
            of old whiskey will have ended here now.

The Arch

Of all living monuments has the fewest
facts attached to it, they slide right off
its surface, no Lincoln lap for them to sit
on and no horse to be astride. Here is what
                        I know for sure:

Was a gift from one city to another. A city
cannot travel to another city, a city cannot visit
any city but itself, and in its sadness it gives
            away a great door in the air. Well
            a city cannot *except for Paris*, who puts
on a hat styled with pigeon wings and walks
through the streets of another city and will not
even see the sights, too full she is of the sights
already. And within her walk her women,
            and the women of Paris looking like
            they just walked through an Arch . . .

Or am I mixing it up I think I am
with another famous female statue? Born
in its shadow and shook-foil hot the facts
slid off me also. I and the Arch we burned
to the touch. 'Don't touch that Arch a boy
we know got third-degree burns from touch-
            ing that Arch,' says my mother sitting
for her statue. She is metal on a hilltop and
so sad she's not a Cross. She was long ago
given to us by Ireland. What an underhand
            gift for an elsewhere to give, a door
that reminds you you can leave it. She raises
            her arm to brush my hair. Oh no female
armpit lovelier than the armpit of the Arch.

When the World Was Ten Years Old
He Fell Deep in Love with Egypt

Just as he fell in love with the dinosaurs,
just as he would fall in love with the moon –
no women in the world yet, he was only ten
years old. A ten-year-old is made of time,
the world had forever to learn about Egypt.
He entered encyclopedias and looted every
fact of them and when he had finished looting
     there he broke into the Bible. He snuck
into his mother's room and drew thick lines
around his eyes and those were the borders
of Egypt. He carefully wrote in stiff small
birds, he carefully wrote in coiled snakes,
he carefully wrote in flatfooted humans.
The ten-year-old world needed so much
privacy, he learned to draw the door-bolt
          glyph and learned to make the sound
          it made. I am an old white British man,
decided the ten-year-old world, I wear a round
lens on my right eye, the Day, and see only a blur
with my left eye, the Night. When the sun shone
on him it shone on Egypt, all the dark for a while
          was the dark in the Pyramids, the left lung
of his body was the shape of Africa
          and one single square breath in it Egypt.
They never found all the tombs, he *knew*. Anyone
might be buried in Egypt, thought the ten-year-old
world in love with it, I will send my wind down
into my valley, and my wind will uncover the doors
to the tombs, and I will go down myself inside them,

and shine light on all the faces, and light on the rooms
full of gold, and light on even the littlest pets, on the mice
and the beetles of the ten-year-old kings, and shine light
on even their littlest names.

List of Cross-Dressing Soldiers

First there was Helen of Sparta, who did it only
with oil, no one knows how; then there was
Maggie of England, who even on the battlefield
put men back together; and then there was Rose
of the deepest South, who stood up in her father's
clothes and walked out of the house and herself.

Disguised women were always among them.
They badly wanted to wear blue, they badly
wanted to wear red, they wanted to blend
        with the woods or ground. Together
with men they were blown from their pronouns.
Their faces too were shot off which were then
free of their bodies. 'I never had any dolls I only
had soldiers. I played soldier from the minute
I was born. Dropped my voice down almost
into the earth, wore bandages where I didn't
need them, was finally discovered by the doctor,
        was finally discovered at the end.'

Someone thought long and hard how to best
make my brother blend into the sand. He came
back and he was heaped up himself like a dune,
he was twice the size of me, his sight glittered
deeper in the family head, he hid among himself,
and slid, and stormed, and looked the same
as the next one, and was hot and gold and some-
        where else.

My brother reached out his hand to me and said,
'They should not be over there. Women should not
be over there.' He said, 'I watched people burn

to death. They burned to death in front of me.'
A week later his red-haired friend killed himself.
And even his name was a boy's name: Andrew.

A friend writes to him, 'My dress blues are being
altered for a bloodstripe.' That's a beautiful line,
I can't help hearing. 'Kisses,' he writes to a friend.
His friend he writes back, 'Cuddles.' Bunch of girls,
bunch of girls. They write each other, 'Miss you,
brother.' Bunch of girls, bunch of girls. They passed
the hours with ticklefights. They grew their mustaches
together. They lost their hearts to local dogs,
                what a bunch of girls.

I sent my brother nothing in the desert because
I was busy writing poems. Deciding one by one
where the breath commas went, or else it would
not stand and walk. This was going to be a poem
about release from the body. This was going
to be a poem about someone else, maybe even me.

My brother is alive because of a family capacity
for little hairs rising on the back of the neck.
The night the roadside bomb blew up, all three
sisters dreamed of him. There, I just felt it,
the family capacity. My brother is alive because
the family head sometimes hears a little voice.

I had been writing the poem before the boy died.
It then did not seem right to mention that burn means
different things in different bodies. I was going
to end the poem with a line about the grass. But

they were in the desert, and I was in the desert when
I thought about them, and no new ending appeared
to me. I was going to write, 'The hill that they died on
was often a woman, wearing the greatest uniform of war,
which is grass.' I know my little brother's head. The scalp
is almost green, where the hair is shortest. I know
my little brother's head, and that is where the ending
lives, the one that sends the poem home, and makes grass
stand up on the back of the neck, and fits so beautiful
         no one can breathe – the last words live
in the family head, and let them live in there a while.

The Hunt for a Newborn Gary

Once babies were born as Garys
and no one doubted what they were, and they were
true men, these babies,

with dangle, and the very name
Gary it had the sound of exposing itself to you. Each
Gary made a fine crowd noise, each Gary was a Crowd
to cheer his death-defying loop-de-loops, and each Gary
went wild when he did not die, one Gary after another
in a loud unbroken line. But was somewhere born a baby
named Gary, sometime in the last fifteen years? Not one,
says the Living Record. Not at two o'clock in the morning,
not at three o'clock in the afternoon, and Gary sounds to us
now the way ORVILLE must have sounded in 1950: a man
in the brand-new days of the car saying Haw and Gee
to his Ford, he can't help it, so recent did the horseflank
twitch beneath the fly. What Garys are still alive are gray,
they ask to hold our newborns and the rest of the family
looks on afraid. If the infants are dropped and broken
they will make a sick overripe sound: Gary. Now just
one minute I interrupt, my father had that name,

I don't believe a word of this, except for the honest
word Gary. When he had it the name was in fullest flower
and perfectly a name of the now, and he shot wiggling
seconds into my mom and one of them plumped and grew
bigheaded, and he named me he couldn't help it Orange,
and my life was a film as long as my life of my name growing
mold in real time. I was part of a picnic basket, and packed
for a family trip, for a family trip to where, the past, and Gary
was a canyon there, and the babies of the past tumbled into him
happily, and the sunset into him was famous, and up and down
his sides grew the freshest wildest four o'clocks.

The Fake Tears of Shirley Temple

How many sets of her parents are dead. How
many times over is she an orphan. A plane,
a crosswalk, a Boer war. A childbirth, of course,
her childbirth. When she, Shirley Temple, came
out of her mother, plump even at her corners
like a bag of goldfish, and one pinhole just one
pinhole necessary. Shirley Temple, cry for us,
and Shirley Temple cried. The first word of no
baby is 'Hello,' how strange. The baby believes,
'I was here before you, learning to wave just
             like the Atlantic.' Alone in the world
just like the Atlantic, and left on a doorstep
just like the Atlantic, wrapped in the grayest,
roughest blanket. Shirley Temple gurgled
and her first words were, 'Your father is lost
at sea.' 'Your mother was thrown by a foam-
colored horse.' 'Your father's round face is
a round set of ripples.' 'Every gull has a chunk
                          of your mom in its beak.'
Shirley Temple what makes you cry. What do
you think of to make you cry. Mommies stand
in a circle and whisper to her. 'Shirley Temple
there will be war. Shirley Temple you'll get no
lunch.' Dry, and dry, and a perfect desert. Then:
          'Shirley Temple your goldfish are dead,
they are swimming toward the ocean even now,'
                          and her tears they fall in black
and white, and her tears they star in the movie.
She cries so wet her hair uncurls, and then the rag
is in the ringlet and the curl is in the wave, she thinks
of dimples tearing out of her cheeks and just running,
out of cheeks knees and elbows and running hard

back to the little creamy waves where they belong,
and the ocean. Her first
          glimpse of the ocean was a fake tear for dad.
A completely filled eye for her unseen dead father,
who when he isn't dead he is gone across the water.

A Recent Transformation Tries to Climb the Stairs

One segment of a worm ago I was a swan,
I stank of the surface of lake just the surface
and I was a sight on the water. Why is it always
the swans, why is it never the stilts who turn
human, the stilts who would know how to walk
at least? I lift my webfoot for once and for all
and I try to climb one step, but a blubbery force-
field surrounds me now and I learn why human
women bounce: they're deeply encased in pink
rubber, so sad. The smell

               of it, erasing! Erasing a picture
of what? Pink Pearl is written everywhere!
A bite mark on one end, a mouth of incisors
and molars and canines – out of nowhere I know
the proper terms, I suddenly want to know every-
thing else, and whenever I felt that way on the lake
I simply ate a fish-head, but fish-heads won't fill

       me now. Your attention is a fish-head,
so throw it back into my new body, back
into the body climbing the stairs. For ten years
writers loved phantom hands and wrote with
and about them nonstop, this particular writer

                     wrote, I quote,
'She lifted her phantom hand and she threw it
to the swans,' but where are all the writers who
had extra hands sewed on? Which hand should
get the pen? The one that never wrote a word
or the one that knows what to do? Is there one
that knows what to do, is this it? A grown girl
swan is called a what, the tips of my fingers

can almost touch it! You'll look it up when you
get home – a recent transformation has no way
        of knowing which wordplays are mostly
exhausted. My hair blows out behind me, where
my hair is attached to my head

                        I can feel a rushing
hot pivot, like where the wind changes direction.
I think that's where I begin to be dead, the best
part of this new body – better to be in one cell
of a swan! When I finally feel where these new
legs end,

                I'll take two at a time to the top
of the stairs and two at a time back down,
and I'll walk to the lake and climb in a swanboat
                        and ride as a gizzard inside it.

The Feeling of Needing a Pen

Really, like a urine but even more gold,
I thought of that line and I felt it, even
between two legs I felt it, the legs I wrote
just now, a panic, a run-walk to the private
                room with a picture of a woman
on the door, or else the line was long, too long,
I barged into the men's, and felt stares burning
hard like reading or noon, felt them looking
me up and over, felt them looking me over
and down, and all the while just holding their
pens,
                they do it different oh no they don't,
they do it standing up, they do it at the window,
they do it so secret in a three-hour bath, they do it
                aloud to someone else, their wife is catching
every word and every word is gold. What you eat
                is in it, blackberries for breakfast are in it,
fat atoms of Shakespeare and Hitler are in it.
The sound of water makes me need to: Atlantic,
Pacific, Caspian, Black. I feel it so much because
I am pregnant, I am pregnant with a little self,
                all of its self
is that spot on a dog that causes its leg to kick.
It kicked and I felt and I wrote that last line. Even
now it's happening. I eat only asparagus like arrows,
I am famous for my aim. I get almost none on my hands,
almost. Under my feet the streets, under the streets
                the pipes. Inside the pipes a babble sound.

Nessie Wants to Watch Herself Doing It

Doing what, I don't know, being alive. The green
of her is a scum on the surface, she would like
to look at herself. Should I have a memory?
she wonders. Of mother washing my frogskin
in muddy water? I do not have that memory.
My near-transparent frogskin? Mother washing
it with mud to keep it visible? I do not have that
memory, almost, almost. Warmblooded though
she knows for a fact, and spontaneously generated
from the sun on stone, and one hundred vertebrae in every
wave of the lake, as one hundred vertebrae in every wave
of her. All of her meat blue rare blue rare, a spot
on her neck that would drive her wild if anyone ever
touched it, and the tip of her tail ends with -ness and
-less. So far all she knows of the alphabet is signs
that say NO SWIMMING.

So far all she knows is her whereabouts.
Has great HATRED for the parochial, does the liver
of the lake. Would like to go to universe . . . al . . . ity?

She has heard there is a good one in Germany.
They stay up all night drinking some black sludge,
and grow long beards rather than look at them-
selves, and do thought experiments like: if I am not
in Scotland, does Scotland even exist? What do I look
like when no one is looking? She would listen to them
just as hard as she could with the mud-sucking holes
in her head – and they, she thinks, would listen back,
with their ears so regularly described as seashell.
The half of her that is underwater would like to be
under a desk, the head of her that is underwater
would like to be fully immersed.

                    I will be different there,
she thinks, with a powerful wake ahead of me.
When will the thinkers come for me. Visited only
here by believers. Is so deep-sea-sick of believers.
When will the thinkers come for me here, where
the green stretches out before me, and I am my own
front lawn. The green is a reflective green, a green
in the juicy shadows of leaves – a *bosky* even green –
a word I will learn to use, and use without self-
consciousness, when at last I go to Germany. I have
holed myself away here, sometimes I am not here
at all, and I feel like the nice clean hole in the leaf
                    and the magnifying glass above me.
She looks to the believers on the shore. A picture
                    it would last longer! shouts Nessie.
Does NOT believe photography can rise to the level
of art, no matter how much rain falls in it, as levels
of the lake they rose to art when Nessie dipped
her body in it. Nessie wants to watch herself doing
it. Doing what, I don't know, being alive. The lake
bought one Nessie and brought her home. She almost
died of loneliness until it gave her a mirror. The lake
could be a mirror, thinks Nessie. Would be perfectly
                    still if I weren't in it.

Bedbugs Conspire to Keep Me from Greatness

In the cities all the poets, and in all the cities,
bedbugs. Fat with their black lyric blood! Alive
at only night, and there and then not there. Better
bedbugs than the ones that eat paper, say poets –
            the ones that eat paper are in our blood
and the bedbugs eat them up, rip rip, and our paper
creamily goes on whole, with not a single real space
between sentences in it. They say come to the cities
and there
            become Great! The poets have money to spend
in the cities: they spend the newest American dollars,
the crisp-aired greenest American dollars, blazing
with pictures of National Parks. 'The Old Faithful
Geyser almost gushes off the note!' At last money admits
the power of poetry, at last money admits it is written
on – and this piece of paper almost gushes, so go to a city
            and spend it. The poets in cities save their money
and travel to National Parks, and never sleep at night
there, no one sleeps in a National Park, they stay up late
and inseminate each other with memories of mountains
and glimpses of wildlife, and human reflections in stilly
chill lakes, and afterward they lie awake, miles away
from any city, miles away from their living mattresses
            where their absent shapes are getting sucked
for their blood. Oh the bedbugs are happy; in bedbug prison,
the locked-up poet is writing his poems, in blood just like
the first time. Oh the poets are happy back in the cities, there
are legible smears on their sheets every day, and a pricking
always on their skin like something is coming
for them through the grass, long green grass
                        of where they came from.

Last of the Late Great Gorilla-Suit Actors

Is the last man alive on this earth. He has the cities
to himself, and even has the blondes, who are over
his shoulders not kicking or screaming. He carries
them wherever he carries the gorilla. 'I can see straight
through and past your mask,' the gorilla-suit actor
tells himself. 'I can see your eyes twinkle way up
with the stars. Between two skyscrapers I can see them.
By the end the audience will recognize you. By the end
they will see you as one of them, by the end they will see
                              their faces in your face,'
          and the audience feels themselves lifted up too,
and the audience leaves one by one. 'Where is the movie,
where is my movie?' the gorilla cries in despair. He beats
his bass chest, there is only silence. He opens his mouth
and makes the loud frightened music the score makes
when we first see him. He is taller than even he remembers.
Comets streak through and through his head. All the blondes
are thrown over his shoulders, the blondes he never even
liked, the bunches of blondes he mistook for bananas. What
he likes is the Chrysler Building, all nipped and shirred
at the waist. What he likes is the cool copper Statue of Liberty.
What he likes, getting bigger, is that high-heeled continent.
What he likes, he thinks, sweat dripping sky to the ground,
is the great gorilla-suit itself and its long great line of inhabitants.
The late great is alone, is alone on the earth. The sun approaches
hotter than hot, the last and screamingest of the blondes.
The last of the great is as big as deep space, the last of the late
is as big as the night, he reaches out and grabs the sun, he is
stuffed with the stars of gorilla-suit acting, all gorilla-suit
actors are moving his arms, all gorilla-suit actors are moving
                    his legs, and we make the sad music the score makes

when the gorilla is shot full of holes, and 'Remember me!'
we cry to no one at large, and burst out of the suit at last
                to breathe, last of the late great gorilla-suit actions.

Factories Are Everywhere in Poetry Right Now

We are watching a crayon being made, we are children,
          we are watching the crayon become crayons
and more crayons and thinking how can there be enough
room in America to make what makes it up, we are thinking
all America is a factory by now, the head of it churning out
          fake oranges, the hand of it churning out glass bottles,
                    the heel of it churning out Lego men.
We are watching lifelike snakes get made, we are watching
lifelike rats get made, we are watching army men get made;
          a whole factory for magic wands, a whole factory
for endless scarves, a whole factory, America, for the making
of the doves, a whole factory, America,
                              for the making of long-eared
rabbits and their love of deep dark holes. We are watching
a marble being made, how does the cat's eye get in the marble
and how does the sight get into that, how does the hand get
on it, how does the hand attach to the child, how does the child
attach to the dirt, and how does the dirt attach to its only name,
America. The name is manufactured here by rows of me in airless
          rooms. Sunlight is accidental, sunlight is runoff
from the lightbulb factory, is ooze on the surface of all our rivers.
Our abandoned factories make empty space and our largest
factory produces distance and its endless conveyor produces miles.
And people in the basement produce our underground. Hillbilly
          teeth are made here, but hillbilly teeth are made everywhere
maybe. The factory that makes us is overseas, and meanwhile we,
America, churn out China, France, Russia, Spain, and our glimpses
of them from across the ocean. Above the factory billowing clouds
          can be seen for miles around. Long line of us never
                              glances up
          from the long line of glimpses we're making, we could make
          those glimpses in the dark, our fingertips could see to do it,

all the flashing fish in the Finger Lakes have extra-plus eyes in America. The last factory, which makes last lines, makes zippers for sudden reveals: a break in the trees opens ziiiip on a view, the last line opens ziiiip on enormous meaning.

Revealing Nature Photographs

　　　　　　　In a field where else you found a stack
of revealing nature photographs, of supernude nature
photographs, split beaver of course nature photographs,
　　　　photographs full of 70s bush, nature taking come
from every man for miles around, nature with come back
　　　　to me just dripping from her lips. The stack came
up to your eye, you saw: nature is big into bloodplay,
nature is into extreme age play, nature does wild inter-
racial, nature she wants you to pee in her mouth, nature
is dead and nature is sleeping and still nature is on all fours,
a horse it fucks nature to death up in Oregon, nature is hot
young amateur redheads, the foxes are all in their holes
for the night, nature is hot old used-up cougars, nature
makes gaping fake-agony faces, nature is consensual dad-
on-daughter, nature is completely obsessed with twins,
nature doing specialty and nature doing niche, exotic females
they line up to drip for you, nature getting paddled as hard
as you can paddle her, oh a whitewater rapid with her ass
　　　　　in the air, high snowy tail on display just everywhere.
The pictures were so many they started to move. Let me
watch for the rest of my natural life, you said and sank down
in the field and breathed hard. Let me watch and watch
without her knowing, let me see her where she can't see me.
As long as she can't see me, I can breathe hard here forever.
See nature do untold animals sex, see nature's Sicko Teeen
Farm SexFeest, see her gush like the geyser at Yellowstone,
see the shocking act that got her banned in fifty-one states including
Canada. See men for miles around give nature what she needs,
rivers and rivers and rivers of it. You exhale with perfect
happiness. Nature turned you down in high school.

　　　　　　　　　　Now you can come in her eye.

See a Furious Waterfall Without Water

Never has an empty hand been made
into more of a fist, and Waterfall Without
        it swings so hard it swings out
of existence. How will anyone get married
now, with no wall of water behind them?
How will Over Niagara Falls in a Barrel
marry Across Niagara Falls on a Tightrope?
Over the Falls would have worn a veil,
Across the Falls would have tied a tie,
hand in hand they would have poured
down the aisle to the sound of rustling
        silks. Later they would narrow
to a lovely neck, later they would make
a gentle elbow in the water, later
they would pour into a still round pool,
and dance for three minutes to what they
called music. Niagara Falls is a family
member. He is drunk for the first time
in a hundred years. 'I don't call that music
I call that noise,' would have screamed
Niagara Falls, right through his aquiline
family nose. All of Niagara's ex-lovers
are here. The World's Steepest Dive
stands up and says, 'I've been diving
        so long now, and when will I hit?
When will you be there for me, Niagara?'
First Woman Behind the Falls stands up
so everyone can see her, so everyone
can see what has happened to her looks.
'You took the best day of my life,
                Niagara.' The World's
                Longest Breath-Hold stands up,

she loves him, she drew in her breath
the first time she saw him and never
breathed out again, not ever. The furious
waterfall without water he punches her
into tomorrow; the World's Longest
Breath-Hold is longer now and she calls
to him from the future, 'You're here,

      you're roaring again where I am,
Tomorrow.' Finally his first love the U-
Shape stands up. Stands up and she says,
'Niagara.' The sound curves down and up
again, even the shape of her voice is a U.
'I don't call that music I call that noise,'
says the furious waterfall without water,
trembling at the very lip, unable to contain
himself, and there he goes roaring

                back into her arms.

Love Poem Like We Used to Write It

Says here is a girl who gets written like palms,
says here is a girl who moves paint like Tahiti.
Teeth infinite white and infinite many and with
them she infinite eat me, and mouth full of invert
and cane and coarse sugar, and her dresses all
came from across
      the water, and they rode a light chop
on the sea in fast ships, and she owns twenty
pairs of the shape of her hands, and slashed silk
on her shoulder like claws of a parrot, and here
the love poem delights:
                the word *parrot* will never
be replaced, and will continue meaning always
exactly what it means, as none of the words
in this sentence have done – come read me again
in a hundred years and see how I keep my shape!
Love poem back to your subject, the word *parrot*
is not the right woman for you, hard to hold
and too much red; love poem think long arms
                and flies nowhere.
I remember her now, it says, and says she is far
from me, says hear how her voice is a Western
slope, when west meant the sun it rose and set
there, and monstrous the shadows of flowers all
down it, in the days before voice meant something
you wrote with. Love poem as we used to write it
says her small brown paw is adorable, which is
to say brown as we used to use it, which is to say
                just sunburned,
just monstrous the shadows of flowers all on it,
which is to say paw as we used to use it, which is
to say a human hand, and human as we used

to use it, which is to say almost no one among us.
Blond of course and blond. Blond as a coil of rope,
and someone hauled on her somewhere, and loop
after loop flew out of her helpless. The someone
was out at sea, and language on my shoulder like
       claws of a parrot. I sailed the world over
to deliver one letter, one letter of even one letter,
one word, and one word as we used to use it:
in those days she was the only Lady, in those days
             she wrote a small round hand,
and I hauled on it saw it fly loop by loop out of her.

Why Haven't You Written

The past, when it was sick right down
to its roses, obsessively checked the mail.
We wore all of our pathways checking
the mail. We went into the woods because
we heard the letters rustling, and we swore
they sounded like letters to us. Even Thoreau,
on Walden Pond, checked his open mouth
every morning, foolishly believing it to be
the mail. We worshipped a great white
body that was an avalanche of good news,
and we slit it open in every part. 'That can't
go through the mail,' the postman gasped,
    'because that is a super-stabbed body!'
The super-stabbed body rose up, with many
butterknives sticking out of it, and said, 'I AM
                the mail.' It had so many lovers.
Everyone alive had a finger in it, ripping it open,
sometimes with blood, deep bleeding wounds
of information all over the back-and-forth form.
It took a long time to be delivered then, and traveled
in sacks like shapes of women, and women were
full of secret sharp corners where their postcards
were poking out, and at last in their bedrooms they
sighed with relief as they shook out their sacks
with both hands, and faithfully and affectionately
and yours tumbled out, and even I am tumbled out.
Most letters were love letters until they were not.
That was when the mail began to change –
and 'enveloped,' the only word that was believed
to contain its meaning, was opened and found to be
empty. Back then it meant something when my letter
never arrived, and now after ten years reaches you,

who are dead or in love with a lookalike, or so full
of hate for me that you can barely see to read this.
If you're not reading this then it never got there,
            and both of us are married to someone else.
The body of the mail still waits for your knife.
            Why haven't you written. Why don't you write.

Rape Joke

The rape joke is that you were nineteen years old.

The rape joke is that he was your boyfriend.

The rape joke it wore a goatee. A goatee.

Imagine the rape joke looking in the mirror, perfectly reflecting back itself, and grooming itself to look more like a rape joke. 'Ahhhh,' it thinks. 'Yes. *A goatee.*'

No offense.

The rape joke is that he was seven years older. The rape joke is that you had known him for years, since you were too young to be interesting to him. You liked that use of the word *interesting*, as if you were a piece of knowledge that someone could be desperate to acquire, to assimilate, and to spit back out in different form through his goateed mouth.

Then suddenly you were older, but not very old at all.

The rape joke is that you had been drinking wine coolers. Wine coolers! Who drinks wine coolers? People who get raped, according to the rape joke.

The rape joke is he was a bouncer, and kept people out for a living.

Not you!

The rape joke is that he carried a knife, and would show it to you, and would turn it over and over in his hands as if it were a book. He wasn't threatening you, you understood. He just really liked his knife.

The rape joke is he once almost murdered a dude by throwing him through a plate-glass window. The next day he told you and he was trembling, which you took as evidence of his sensitivity.

How can a piece of knowledge be stupid? But of course you were so stupid.

The rape joke is that sometimes he would tell you you were going on a date and then take you over to his best friend Peewee's house and make you watch wrestling while they all got high.

The rape joke is that his best friend was named Peewee.

OK, the rape joke is that he worshipped The Rock.

Like the dude was completely in love with The Rock. He thought it was so great what he could do with his eyebrow.

The rape joke is he called wrestling 'a soap opera for men.' Men love drama too, he assured you.

The rape joke is that his bookshelf was just a row of paperbacks about serial killers. You mistook this for an interest in history, and laboring under this misapprehension you once gave him a copy of Günter Grass's *My Century*, which he never even tried to read.

It gets funnier.

The rape joke is that he kept a diary. I wonder if he wrote about the rape in it.

The rape joke is that you read it once, and he talked about another girl. He called her Miss Geography, and said 'he didn't have those urges when he looked at her anymore,' not since he met you. Close call, Miss Geography!

The rape joke is that he was your father's high school student – your father taught World Religion. You helped him clean out his classroom at the end of the year, and he let you take home the most beat-up textbooks.

The rape joke is that he knew you when you were twelve years old. He once helped your family move two states over, and you drove from Cincinnati to St. Louis with him, all by yourselves, and he was kind to you, and you talked the whole way. He had chaw in his mouth the entire time, and you told him he was disgusting and he laughed, and spat the juice through his goatee into a Mountain Dew bottle.

The rape joke is that *come on*, you should have seen it coming. This rape joke is practically writing itself.

The rape joke is that you were facedown. The rape joke is you were wearing a pretty green necklace that your sister had made for you. Later you cut that necklace up. The mattress felt a specific way, and your mouth felt a specific way open against it, as if you were speaking, but you know you were not. As if your mouth were open ten years into the future, reciting a poem called Rape Joke.

The rape joke is that time is different, becomes more horrible and more habitable, and accommodates your need to go deeper into it.

Just like the body, which more than a concrete form is a capacity.

You know the body of time is *elastic*, can take almost anything you give it, and heals quickly.

The rape joke is that of course there was blood, which in human beings is so close to the surface.

The rape joke is you went home like nothing happened, and laughed about it the next day and the day after that, and when you told people you laughed, and that was the rape joke.

It was a year before you told your parents, because he was like a son to them. The rape joke is that when you told your father, he made the sign of the cross over you and said, 'I absolve you of your sins, in the name of the Father, and of the Son, and of the Holy Spirit,' which even in its total wrongheadedness was so completely sweet.

The rape joke is that you were crazy for the next five years, and had to move cities, and had to move states, and whole days went down into the sinkhole of thinking about why it happened. Like you went to look at your backyard and suddenly it wasn't there, and you were looking down into the center of the earth, which played the same red event perpetually.

The rape joke is that after a while you weren't crazy anymore, but close call, Miss Geography.

The rape joke is that for the next five years all you did was write, and never about yourself, about anything else, about apples on the tree, about islands, dead poets and the worms that aerated them, and there was no warm body in what you wrote, it was elsewhere.

The rape joke is that this is finally artless. The rape joke is that you do not write artlessly.

The rape joke is if you write a poem called Rape Joke, you're asking for it to become the only thing people remember about you.

The rape joke is that you asked why he did it. The rape joke is he said he didn't know, like what else would a rape joke say? The rape joke said YOU were the one who was drunk, and the rape joke said you remembered it wrong, which made you laugh out loud for one long split-open second. The wine coolers weren't Bartles & Jaymes, but it would be funnier for the rape joke if they were. It was some pussy flavor, like Passionate Mango or Destroyed Strawberry, which you drank down without question and trustingly in the heart of Cincinnati, Ohio.

Can rape jokes be funny at all, is the question.

Can any part of the rape joke be funny. The part where it ends – haha, just kidding! Though you did dream of killing the rape joke for years, spilling all of its blood out, and telling it that way.

The rape joke cries out for the right to be told.

The rape joke is that this is just how it happened.

The rape joke is that the next day he gave you *Pet Sounds*. No really. *Pet Sounds*. He said he was sorry and then he gave you *Pet Sounds*. Come on, that's a little bit funny.

Admit it.

The Hornet Mascot Falls in Love

Piece human, piece hornet, the fury
of both, astonishing abs all over it.
Ripped, just ripped to absolute bits,
his head in the hornet and his head
in the hum, and oh he want to sting
     her. The air he breathes is filled
with flying cheerleader parts. Splits
flips and splits, and ponytails in orbit,
the calm eye of the panty in the center
of the cartwheel, the word HORNETS
– how? – flying off the white uniform.
Cheerleaders are a whole, are known
to disassemble in the middle of the air
and come back down with different
thighs, necks from other girls, a lean
gold torso of Amber-Ray on a bubbling
bottom half of Brooke. The mouths that
cry GOOD HANDS GOOD HANDS.
The arms he loves that make the basket,
the body he loves that drops neat
                    into them.
Oh the hybrid human and hornet, who
     would aim for pink balloons.
Oh the swarm of Cheerleading Entity,
who with their hivemind understand
him. Rhyme about the hornet, *her* tongue
in *her* mouth at the top of *her* throat! Clap
one girl's hand against another's. Even
            exchange screams in the air.
The pom-poms, fact, are flesh. Hornet
Mascot is hungry, and rubs his abs, where
the hornet meets the man. Wants to eat

and hurl a honey, in the middle
of the air. (No that is bees I'm thinking of.
Like I ever went to class, when the show
was all outside.) The hornet begins to fly
toward the cheerleaders. 'Make me
the point of your pyramid,' he breathes.
And they take him up in the air with them
and mix and match his parts with theirs,
and all come down with one gold stripe,

    and come down sharp and stunned,
and lie on the ground a minute, all think-
ing am I dead yet, where am I, did we win.

The Descent of the Dunk

First no one could dunk and then they all could.
The dunk evolved, and then stood upright, was even
perceived to be intelligent, with too big a brain
at the top of it, the ball. It grew upright and smooth-
skinned with a tendency toward religion, the dunk
stood up too fast, they said, and consequently has
headaches, and trouble breathing in spring when
it is so beautiful. The childhood of the dunk
                              was no childhood at all.
He practiced on a paper route, throwing *The Sun*
to the same place each morning. Did not sleep long
but when he slept, the springs of his bed imparted
something to him. At night the streetlight floated
down and let him dribble it. Then there was school
there was every day school where he crumpled up
tests and tossed them in the trashcan. He shouted
TWO POINTS and had to stay after and copy out
the 'football' page of the dictionary, which could not
keep him down – he saw writers of the dictionary
at their desks, performing small silent neat dunks.
The crowd of the devoted watching. Like watching
is reading. Like it isn't. The dunk felt like a leather
study in space, and someone thinking *how* inside him,
and a perfected body in a leather chair wondering just
how high he can jump toward heaven. A leap sometimes
occurs within an animal, the dunk felt that happen
within him. He landed sure on his feet again and then
he was wholly himself. A joint so surely in its socket,
the whole city could go walking on it. All the rain
comes down at once in a single bounding drop,
and the wells of the countryside look up at once full,
and no open mouth is thirsty, and every mouth is open.

A great heavy body it weighed the dunk down. The dunk
and the moon pulled it up like the sea. The crowd of us
shouted his name to dunk him deep into himself. More
than half-moons in his fingertips, and rising through the air
in a loud round translation,
        and the air right then breathing him back.
Was the only complete thing in the world, was the dunk.
        Well that and everyone who watched it.
Goosebumps even on the ball. The ball spinning like
bodies could live on it, and whatever led up to the bodies
too. It stood up too fast, it got taller and taller, its women get
bellies like basketballs. A woman dunking! That'll be the day.
Yet here I am sailing over your heads, and then,
                with the sound, slamming into them.

The Third Power

Little boy he is learning to see
Magic Eyes. Little boy hidden objects
leap out their way at him. He covers
his walls with the pink and red posters,
and pops his black eyes at them, and sees
all the objects that live in the sun, objects
so tan they stand out against sand. More
than words the boy wants to see something
undress, even if only a lake and a sailboat.
They jump out and he longs to jump in –
he would cannonball into that lake and
just float. Here he is in a room that smells
all locked up, like men and the imprisonment
of lizards, and he stares at Magic Eyes,
in fact he stares so hard it hurts, and says
oh my God a heart, and oh my God a pair
of lips, because what is 3-D after all? When
the air in the room becomes apparent,
and carves itself out around a her or a him,
and now little boy's father he bangs down
the door, and strides in and stares so hard
that he hurts, says, 'We had 3-D in my day
and we called it AMERICA! We had 3-D
in my day and we called it bare bosoms!'
but the pictures refuse to open for him

or show even their innocent parts:
the dog and the sphere and the American
flag will never undress

for the first time again.
He slams the door behind him, and thinks

getting into heaven is hard. It is the cube
that does not open. It is the cube that is only
to look at, but look. There behind that door, look
there. There the cube is, leaping out of the square.

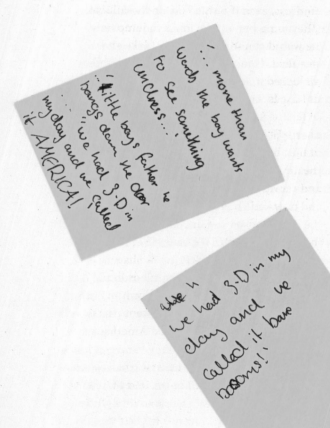

Natural Dialogue Grows in the Woods

Along with the poison berries,
and it's your job in this life to spit both out,
and spit both out if you want to live. Listen
and learn to me and the woods: the Ummm
of the little crickets. The fresh and slangy
crows, who end every last word with the letter
A. Rats, say the mice in the woods, and What's
the fuckin difference, Dad? My PawPaw
always says, says the voice inside the fruit tree.
Good ears and great ears and even uncanny
are trembling here in the woods, perked every-
where are ears for speech as it is spoke. Stiffies
of dialogue circle the trees and look for holes
in the conversation, and wait to get Red Riding
Hood as soon as she leaves the wild.
She says she never will, and stretches the word
giiiiiiiiiiiiiiiiiiiiiiiiiiirl so long that we all become
women during it. The woodsman lives here too,
and he stretches the word maaaaaaaaaaaaaaaan
so long that we all die out before he's done.
Death is so random, deep here in the woods.
In the woods the eternal Daaaaaamn and Gonna,
and the small exact birds saying What it is. Like
like like from morning to night, till even the night
is like the day. Nothing dwindles down to nothin.
Maaaaaaaaaaan and giiiiiiiiiiiiiiirl flee to the woods
to forget their proper usage, and after what seems
like endless fuckin – well you know and you know
and you know what I'm saying. Know what
I'm saying and know what I mean. They fall hard
to the grass like the oldest trees and lie a while
listening, and then begin to speak, their mouths full

of the air of natural dialogue: Hopefully, hopefully,
totally, totally. Where are you from I have nowhere
to be. What are you called can I axe you a question.

Can we stay here forever. Probably, probably.
With the probly and the prolly and the loblolly pines.

The Brave Little _____ Goes to School

A–Z animals hunger for learning. They hunger
for learning, you sneak them to school. A mouse
in your pocket, a frog in your pocket. They talk
or you think they can talk. A cricket hides in the dark
of your desk and glitters like a great black IQ point.
You carried a housefly to school in your fist, now
repeat after me the teacher says and the fly makes
vowel sounds one by one and sometimes *y* the
fly says. Now what other animal goes to school –
     a nude in your pocket, a full page of nude!
She shines with concentration all over her skin, trying
so hard to learn to learn. Man is an animal too says
teacher; you brought a man to school today. A man
     from the past is visiting you and the one place
he wanted to go was school and his name is Benjamin
Franklin, Ben. He sits at the desk next to yours, learning
each little quote he's going to say and then lavishing
the learn of his eyes on the nude, whose skin is bursting
with the exports of Ecuador, mostly and mainly rain.
     Ben Franklin should not be in school, the word
in his mouth should not be in school, a word that is where
a girl pees from. A fresh sheet of ditto is laid on your desk.
Don't worry, you tell Ben Franklin – the unlearningest
     animal of all, the Answers, came to school today
in your closed left fist, curly-tailed like they taught you
to write them, impossibly small and already bleeding.
The teacher writes QUIET PLEASE on the board. The pig
who came to school today is unprepared for the squeal
of chalk. It asks is something else in here dying the way
I'm going to? The cricket and Ben Franklin raise their hands,
          the Answers somehow raises yours.

There Were No New Colors for Years

Before neon came along, was made, did not grow
like the rest of the colors, or grew as a tumorous
growth on Art
              wherever sun touched it too much,
and we went to see that tumor in museums
         whenever our parents would take us
and brought replicas home from the gift
       shop – before neon there wasn't a way
to buy plastic packs of plastic stars and put
            the Big Dipper on your ceiling,

        no way to put stars on your ceiling at all
unless you went outside and slept there
     which we stopped doing years before
     when all adults woke up and wanted
      to touch a firm camper between the legs –
it was a new kind of fruit like the maraschino
     and they craved it every minute of the day –
so we stayed indoors and reflected the glow and
all adults were jealous, they turned old-timey shades
of green and they hated our head-to-toe neon,
because:
              The names were the same just
with NEON before them like colors woke freshly
divorced
         and demanded that people call them Ms.,
this made parents uncomfortable and sexually helpless,
they pictured nipples like eyes on stalks, they thought
why was I born too late, and thought how much scarier
it would have been when Orson Welles lied about aliens
          if they'd been able to see neon
in their minds back then, and they banged the doors

angry on their sleeping children, no doubt dreaming
neon dreams that would have killed the parents
with how scary they were, so hard the biggest stars
fell down
                          and fell into our mouths, and we woke
in the morning tasting them, and the stars tasted
                                      toxic and perfectly new.

Perfect Little Mouthfuls

What have we dumped in the ocean? All
the dolphins have begun growing breasts.
Now dolphins are women when you want
women and fish when you want fish,
 at last. The breasts
 they are more playful
than the rest of the dolphin put together!
No nipples according to us, the nipples
the brains of the breast, if the dolphins
had nipples their intelligence *we think*
would add up to more than our own.
Men of the world
 rejoice, it is no longer girly
to own a calendar of dolphins, bursting
the surface of the water and themselves,
thickly spread with the glitter of nature.
Time to turn to the next luscious month –
it's the sluttiest one, April, all covered
with droplets of spring. People who suffer
from extra desire can pay one hundred dollars
to ride them, fifty dollars extra if you want
them to leap, seventy-five if you want them to dive
so deep all the blood rushes into your ears,
and they fill with the crackling sound of sea-
foam. A triangle pokes above the water
and says better shapes below – circles are
the most sought-after shapes of course
but teardrops are also accepted.
 In a childhood room of the Pacific,
a mother gets a glimpse of her mutating daughter
and deeply indraws a gasp of sea. 'I thought

you would stay a dolphin forever!' she cries
out to the blue at large. Who could have seen
this coming? On Minoan jugs all the dolphins
stare knowingly. Dolphins you swim so often
through literature, now we will see even more
of you. Quick pour glowing runoff into the water
and add nipples the brains to the breasts, why not,
now dolphins will be smarter than all of us, we think,
smart enough to read

                              this even, quick pour glowing
runoff into the water, let's give them a fresh new pair
of eyes to read this and read their new run-on with.

The Father and Mother of American Tit-Pics

The father and mother of American poetry are back from the dead for just one day. They are standing up out of their graves, turning to each other, exchanging their tit-pics, and then retreating back into the earth and their silence, and the handfuls of dust all over them that were not their tits at all.

Thank God they were able to do this, or we might never have known what the tits of them looked like.

When you want to say a poet is mysterious, say, 'Very few tit-pics of him exist,' or 'Reading his letters and journals, we are able to piece together a pic of his tits – they loved butter and radishes and were devoted to his sister.'

Neither of the poets were Transcendentalists, but their tit-pics rose up and floated over all, and filled up the sky with rose-colored clouds.

I admit that I brought them back from the dead because I was standing in front of the mirror taking picture after picture of my tits in order to establish for once and all time what a tit actually looks like, since according to the dictionary lots of things can be a tit, even including a bird and an idiot.

'I have birds and idiots all over my body, but not where my pecs are,' I shouted. I was furious. 'Let me set down the meaning of the tit, and get the last word on it.'

Commence me taking hundreds of boob photos, and studying them closely, and thinking most of these don't even look like boobs.

They look like birds and idiots.

And I thought, 'This is not something Emily Dickinson would have done. Or is it.'

Emily Dickinson was the father of American poetry and Walt Whitman was the mother, suckling grizzled wild dogs at his teats.

Walt Whitman nude in the forest, staring deep into a still pool, the only means of taking tit-pics available at that time.

Too many people fell in and drowned, in that age before we learned to really swim in the tit-pic.

Raindrops fell into the still pool of the tit-pic, rippling it outward and jiggling it, since the jiggle within the tit-pic is what we're really after.

The wild dogs they grew up and grew tame, and learned to be owned by American poets, and take them for walks around lakes, as a poet isn't happy unless he is walking in a circle with the double meaning of the word *tit* just bouncing away on his chest.

And meaning on the writing wobbling there like Walt Whitman's tits on the lake, how beautiful, almost like a part of nature.

Walt Whitman with a bra on his head, which is keeping his thoughts from being totally bare. The bra is too small and the bra is made of lace and his friends are saying, 'Walt you are falling OUT' and 'Wow Walt you are giving everyone a show' and 'Why are you giving away the cow for free when I only wanted to hear the moo.'

The boys when looking at Walt Whitman would nudge each other and say 'A body like that could never drown.'

Meaning I guess that his boobs would float him? Or that his lungs were really big so there had to be a lot of breath in them? I never really understood that one.

Or when he was riding the ferry and leaning over to look at the glittering river the boys would nudge each other and holler, 'Careful not to tip over with those huge jugs Walt!' But wouldn't his huge jugs just scoop up the water till the river was dry, and then he would go walking home on the riverbed with his triumphant jugs balanced in front of him threatening to spill but not spilling a drop and even the glitter still intact in them?

The gulf between a word and what it represents is still so great, but a shocking reflection of perfect tits floats and will always float there.

What I am TRYING to say is that metaphors are dangerous!

If teeth are like pearls, and if skin is like a pearl, and if the gates of heaven were twelve pearls, imagine the pearl explosion that would happen if someone bit their own boob in the afterlife.

Which we have to assume Walt Whitman is doing, to make St. Peter upset, which is not very mature, but I'll tell you what IS mature, Walt Whitman's incredible boobs.

I mean he's had two hundred years to develop them.

Perhaps that's why breasts have gotten bigger, because American poetry is accumulating in our lungs and has to push its way out somehow.

But back to how metaphors are dangerous.

When he is old his boobs will seem to him like raindrops trickling down and attempting to join a larger body of water. Thank goodness they are trickling down a window so all of us can see it happen, and we are a girl and we're reading a book as the human rain pours relentlessly down.

Emily Dickinson for instance the father of American poetry is reading Shakespeare there just through the window, and her own body is so fierce and so hot that any droplets that landed there would instantly burn up.

Emily has a beautiful black-and-white beard that reaches down to the ground, and lightning streaks zigzag out of her mouth.

(This is disputed by her photographs, but her photographs know nothing and half of them aren't even her.)

The beard flows over her chest and to look at it is literacy, since the handwriting found in the beards of the past was so curling and flourishing and so feminine, everyone could read it.

When she trims the beard the trimmings fall onto the page and never move again except the dashes, which rearrange themselves in the night.

We have thought two things about her – one that she was a little woman-prune and two that she was an almost mentally overripe plum that was bursting all over the place and calling the wasps to it.

The general assumption has been that HER tit-pics would not be worth looking at if they existed at all, which is false, since I have secret information that they were actually four-dimensional and measured in minutes rather than cups, and wouldn't you like to get a load of those deep and boundless pools of time.

Though maybe you think time doesn't exist, and that's where you got the idea that she was unblessed in the boob department.

What I'm saying is that her boobs were so big they were practically geological ages, and the beard of Father Time flowed over them.

The reason she always wore a white dress, for instance, is so that men would every minute be aware of the soft mounds of time shining through them.

'Eyes up here buddy,' she would say, when their eyes drifted down and lingered on the white and pulsing handfuls of time, and beheld them with huge hunger to touch all the little milliseconds at once.

'Wow, disrespectful!' she once shouted when Stephen Crane burst into her house and grabbed a fistful of her and then dropped dead, too young to hold so much heart-stopping boob of existence in his hand.

Tits roam the earth in search of a body, and they knock on
Emily Dickinson's door, but we'll never know what they
said to each other, and the sound of the knocker itself was
so soft.

The ideal tit would be so big that it would include everything
else in it, and you would be part of it, and you would be
surrounded by it, and it would be wet and nude and in a white
bikini that was see-through enough to show you, and leave
nothing of you to the imagination, right down to the
goosebumps you got in church.

IS IT COLD IN HERE men shout to the boob that contains
them. CAREFUL NOT TO PUT MY EYE OUT WITH
THAT THING they shout to the boob that contains them just
before the darkness closes over.

There is felt to be a huge heartbeat just beyond them.

On her deathbed, Emily Dickinson whispered, 'Destroy the
negatives of my tit-pics, the ones where they look like moon-
rocks, or else people will think I was from outer space.'

Her ideas are often spoken of as being 'out to here,' accompanied
by an exaggerated juggy motion of the hands.

The hands bounced up and down slowly to imply heaviness.

Picture her hidden breast, and a shocking tanline on it,
from even she knows not where, from a sun inside her dress.

Who is not an atheist about Emily Dickinson's body, which is totally unbelievable. It is the Number One Beach Body every year, for the way the letters wash up on it.

Walt Whitman is the Number Two Beach Body every year, because look at the way he snapped back into shape only months after giving birth to American Poetry.

In order to sing louder, pretend you are singing to someone across the room. In order to get bigger tits, pretend they are five minutes ahead of you into the future.

Pretend that more than the rest of you they move around the sun.

'Mommy!' cried the men to the boobs of Emily Dickinson. 'Did someone say Mommy,' Walt Whitman shouted, kicking open the door of his body and running into the room of hers.

'I am the dad here,' Emily Dickinson said gracefully, rearranging the black-and-white curls of her beard.

'I'm the goddamn mom,' Walt Whitman bellowed, detaching a dog from one of his breasts and throwing it into the crowd, where it woofed tremendously among the sexists.

They exactly exchanged their gazes.

'Well, time to die,' Walt Whitman and Emily Dickinson said to each other, and they fell backward at exactly the same moment, toppled at last by their tits, which stood upright with nipples like perfect pink erasers.

Both of them naked, and arrayed in all the invisible words, like said and just and and and oh, which are there but the reader never sees them.

Above them floating their tit-pics.

And floating above their tit-pics our eyes.

The Hypno-Domme Speaks, and
Speaks and Speaks

I was born as a woman, I talk you to death,
                              or else your ear off,
or else you to sleep. What do I have, all the time
in the world, and a voice that swings brass back
and forth, you can hear it, and a focal point where
my face should be. What do I have, I have absolute
power, and what I want is your money, your drool,
and your mind, and the sense of myself as a snake,
and a garter in the grass. Every bone in the snake
is the hipbone, every part of the snake is the hips.
The first sound I make is silence, then ssssshhh,
              the first word I say is listen. Sheepshearers
                        and accountants hypnotize the hardest,
and lookout sailors who watch the sea, and the boys
who cut and cut and cut and cut and cut the grass.
The writers who write page-turners, and the writers
who repeat themselves. The diamond-cutter kneels
down before me and asks me to hypnotize him, and
I glisten at him and glisten hard, and listen to me and
listen, I tell him. Count your age backward, I tell him.
Become aware of your breathing, and aware of mine
              which will go on longer. Believe you
        are a baby till I tell you otherwise, then believe
you're a man till I tell you you're dirt. When a gunshot
rings out you'll lie down like you're dead. When you
        hear, 'He is breathing,' you'll stand up again.
The best dog of the language is Yes and protects you.
The best black-and-white dog of the language is Yes
and goes wherever you go, and you go where I say,
you go anywhere. Why do I do it is easy, I am working
my way through school. Give me the money

for Modernism, and give me the money
for what comes next. When you wake to the fact that you
have a body, you will wake to the fact that not for long.
When you wake you will come when you read the word
hard, or hard to understand me, or impenetrable poetry.
When you put down the book you will come when you
hear the words put down the book,

                                you will come when you hear.

ACKNOWLEDGEMENTS

Thanks to the editors of the following publications, where some of these poems first appeared:

AGNI
The Awl
Colorado Review
Denver Quarterly
Fence
Gulf Coast
Hazlitt
The London Review of Books
The New Yorker
North American Review
PEN Poetry Series
Poetry
A Public Space
Slate
Tin House

Martin Walker got a first in History at Oxford, has worked in Africa as a journalist, lectured in America and served on the campaign staff of Senator Ed Muskie. Since 1971 he has worked on the *Guardian*, has written a book on the National Front and a novel, *The Infiltrator*. His work has appeared in the *New York Times*, the *Washington Post* and *Private Eye*. He lives in London.

Martin Walker

Daily Sketches

A Cartoon History of British Twentieth-Century Politics

PALADIN
GRANADA PUBLISHING
London Toronto Sydney New York

Published by Granada Publishing Limited
in Paladin Books 1978

ISBN 0 586 08270 0

First published by Frederick Muller 1978
Copyright © Martin Walker 1978

Granada Publishing Limited
Frogmore, St Albans, Herts AL2 2NF
and
3 Upper James Street, London WIR 4BP
1221 Avenue of the Americas, New York, NY 10020, USA
117 York Street, Sydney, NSW 2000, Australia
100 Skyway Avenue, Toronto, Ontario, Canada M9W 3A6
110 Northpark Centre, 2193, Johannesburg, South Africa
CML Centre, Queen and Wyndham, Auckland 1, New Zealand

Printed in Great Britain by
Richard Clay (The Chaucer Press) Ltd
Bungay, Suffolk

Set in Monophoto Ehrhardt

for my god-daughter, Rachel

ACKNOWLEDGEMENTS

This book could not have been prepared without the indefatigable and imaginative work of my research collaborator, Susan Morgan. I am also deeply grateful to Dr Graham Thomas, whose Centre for the Study of Cartoons and Caricature at the University of Kent has already saved many thousands of original cartoons for posterity, and who has begun to establish a serious academic framework around the hitherto anarchic mass of cartoon studies. His advice and his personal collection were of enormous value to me, and any merits this book may possess are largely his and Miss Morgan's.

The Editor gratefully acknowledges permission to publish original cartoon material from the following: Punch Publications Ltd; The Daily Telegraph Ltd; Beaverbrook Newspapers Ltd; John Murray Publishers Ltd; Army Information Services; Syndication International Ltd; the Observer; Co-operative Press Ltd; Associated Newspapers Group Ltd; Pressdram Ltd; Guardian Newspapers Ltd; Socialist Worker Publications; The Morning Star; the Transport and General Workers Union; New Masses Publications.

Every effort has been made to trace the owners of the copyright material in this book. It is the Editor's belief that all necessary permissions have been obtained, but in the case of any question arising as to the use of any material, the Editor will be pleased to make the necessary correction in future issues of the book.

INTRODUCTION

When I buy a copy of the *Evening Standard*, I skim the front page headlines and immediately turn to the editorial page for JAK's cartoon. On Monday mornings, the first thing I read in the *Guardian* is John Kent's Varoomshka strip cartoon. Addicted though I may be to my daily fix of newsprint, it is the cartoonist's needle that I crave first. And in buses and on tube trains, in offices and at news-stands, it is clear that there are a lot of us cartoon junkies around.

The fees alone suggest the cartoonist's importance. When David Low joined the *Guardian* in 1953, he was hired at a salary considerably higher than those of the editor or the paper's managing director. In 1933, Sydney Strube was offered £10,000 by the *Daily Herald* to leave the *Daily Express*. Beaverbrook instantly matched the *Herald*'s offer. In 1913, Will Dyson was working for the impoverished radical *Daily Herald* for £5 a week. He was offered ten times that wage by the Hearst syndicate in the US, and the *Herald* launched a special fund to retain him, and managed to raise his wage to £20. Going back further still, one contemporary of Gillray, whose cartoon engravings depicted the Napoleonic Wars, related that the only way to get into the bookshop where they were sold was to fight your way through the crowd with your fists.

Cartoons have a long tradition. Pedants could trace it back to the Bayeux tapestry, if they chose to apply Professor Sir Ernst Gombrich's definition that the cartoon's job is to 'solidify the elusive flux of events into a manageable or memorable myth'.[1] But cartoons as we know them today have a tradition that is part of the social revolution of mass literacy, mass media and a common national pool of knowledge about politicians and the great events of the day. Until late in the nineteenth century, the technology of printing was barely equipped to reproduce cartoons. In the *Punch* of the 1840s, the cartoons were printed from wood engravings, and up to six engravers would work on preparing each cartoon for publication. In 1886, just two years before Francis Carruthers Gould became the first staff cartoonist to be hired by a daily paper, the halftone block was developed and was to launch the distinguished tradition of the press photographer. Ten years later, Harmsworth founded the *Daily Mail*. The staff cartoonist, the new printing technology and the popular press were all cubs from the same litter.

And a very well-behaved litter it was. Until Will Dyson began to draw the bold, radical lines of his own socialist commitment in the *Daily Herald*, cartoonists were on the whole restrained and respectful creatures. They tended to express a smug Victorian complacency in the virtues of thrift, patriotism, the glories of the British Empire and the integrity of its statesmen. The master of this school was *Punch*'s Sir John Tenniel, the man who made the proud lion into the national symbol, and the cartoonist who began the tradition of drawing nations as hefty Grecian matrons. Britannia, Germania, Columbia and Francia cast noble glances from his pages. 'He was discretion itself in producing powerful cartoons that offended nobody ... he was Dignity, not Impudence', wrote David Low.[2] As the Prime Minister, Arthur Balfour, said at a dinner to mark Tenniel's retirement in 1901, 'I do not believe that the satire of that journal (*Punch*) has ever left a wound.'[3] Few cartoonists today would glow under such a judgment from a politician.

Francis Carruthers Gould was proud to recall, 'I etch with vinegar, not vitriol', even though his patent partisanship for the Liberal Party led him to hunt the Liberal renegade Jo Chamberlain in over a hundred caricatured guises after Chamberlain became a Conservative-Unionist.[4] Dog, fox, weasel, donkey – Chamberlain's sharp features were stuck on to all of them. And yet Chamberlain lovingly collected all of Carruthers Gould's cartoons, and told his friends that they meant more than his famed collection of orchids.

This combination of human face with animal body has become an accepted technique since the day of Carruthers Gould. Churchill was delighted to be portrayed as a flying bulldog by *Punch* in the Second World War. It is a technique which spread far beyond cartoons. In *Strike*, one of the early works of the Russian film director Eisenstein, there is a sequence when the faces of the police spies change back and forth from human to animal, to fox, to owl, to cat. In the cinema, the effect is more than disconcerting; it is surreal. In cartoons, we now accept it as an artistic convention. Mussolini was regularly pictured as a cur, crawling at Hitler's heels by British cartoonists before and during the war. And in the 1960s, Cummings regularly portrayed the West German leader Konrad Adenauer as a dachshund, and the effect was neither cruel nor ridiculous. It labelled Adenauer as a German, but one gets the impression that Cummings used the dachshund because of the length of its body – and the long low line became the basis for the composition of his cartoon.

The growth of this technique leads us to the way cartoonists mine each other's ideas, not in the sense of plagiarism, but in recycling ideas and, sometimes, even recycling whole cartoons. The famous Tenniel cartoon of Bismarck's retirement in 1890, called *Dropping the Pilot*, was to be used again by *Punch* sixty years later, to illustrate the ending of British rule in Egypt. Vicky would occasionally plunder the drawings of his predecessors and put modern politicians in a dated but familiar setting. Both Strube and Vicky used Tenniel's old device of drawing a scene from Lewis Carroll's poem *The Walrus and the Carpenter*. Today, Garland exploits old poems, songs and children's stories, to convey a complex re-interpretation of a political character. Perhaps his most successful idea was to draw the Labour and Conservative leadership as two gangs of little boys, based on Richmal Crompton's *William* books. He caught the pettiness of much political debate, the ritual of parliamentary warfare, and drew a subtle class distinction between the Labour rough kids and the Tory private school boys.

But this is the essence of the cartoonist's humour; the placing of familiar, much-respected figures into an environment which illuminates and re-interprets them. Part of the function of humour is to surprise us by bringing together and reconciling disparate elements. To portray Harold Wilson as the leader of a mischievous gang of boys is funny in itself, when the details of the short trousers and the drooping socks and tousled hair are added to the familiar Wilson face. Or take McAllister's German invasion of Britain in 1974 – 'A last desperate attempt to revive the Dunkirk spirit.' It takes the politician's ploy of harking back to the great days, to the indomitable spirit of British fortitude, and shows how our own history is dragooned into a justification of a current Government policy. McAllister just stretches the politician's ploy into the realm of the absurd.

But are cartoons, political cartoons, meant to be funny? Some cartoonists, like Dyson the Socialist ideologue, or Raemaekers the anti-Hun propagandist, clearly have other objectives. JAK, consistently one of the funniest of the political artists, is a master of slapstick cartoons – the Cabinet Minister with the demolished home, the London restaurant whose house wine scorches a devastating track through table, floor and palate. Phil Evans's brilliant summation of the Miners' Strike – based on the classic slapstick idea of the truncated speech – works in a similar, simple way. But humour in a political cartoon is a bonus, rather than something we expect by right. The political cartoonist is not only making a personal comment on the news and its personalities, he is part of a continuous process of debate. Simply by commenting daily or weekly, he builds among his readers an expectation, a preconception if you like, of that cartoonist's political principles and prejudices. His vision becomes a fixed point in a changing political world. In the 1930s, readers were confident enough of Low's approval of the idea of collective security that they could almost predict an attack on Hitler, or a mournful cartoon of the betrayed League of Nations, as soon as a crisis arose.

So with cartoonists like Low, we come to expect a predictable response to political events. But almost all cartoonists quickly develop and fix a visual image of particular politicians.

A relationship can grow between a politician and a cartoonist that is almost symbiotic in its intensity. The classic example is that of Vicky and Harold Macmillan. Intending satire, Vicky drew him as 'Supermac', an aged Superman with inflated shoulders, buck teeth and sad, hang-dog eyes. The nickname stuck, but it stuck in nicely, so that the Supermac nickname became one of Macmillan's major assets in the 1959 General Election.

Cartoonists can wield an awesome power. In spite of press photographs and television, it is probably true to say that the average voter's mental image of the politicians he votes for is an image filtered through the imagination of the popular cartoonists. Politicians are a vulnerable breed. Their calling tends to keep them isolated from the ordinary life of the voter, and a sharp cartoon, showing how others see them, has all the force of that old slave who always rode behind Roman Emperors when they drove through the streets in triumph, whispering into the Emperor's ear, 'Remember, you are only a man.' Stanley Baldwin used to value Low's cartoons about his Ministers as valuable ammunition against the pretensions of his own Cabinet, even though he loathed the cartoonist's work. He once confided to Arthur Christiansen of the *Daily Express* that Low might be a genius, but 'he is evil and malicious.'[5] Churchill went further, coldly informing Lord Beaverbrook in 1940 that Low was 'a Communist of the Trotskyite variety'.[6]

But the reaction of politicians to the work of cartoonists, and the influence which cartoonists exert are two very different things. I doubt whether we will ever measure the effect of specific cartoons. The main guide we have is the untrustworthy one of the way Governments believe cartoonists exercise power. In the 1930s, the Government tried to persuade Low to soften his attacks on Hitler and Mussolini, on the grounds that it made diplomacy more difficult. In the 1940s, the Government tried to minimize the impact of Low's Colonel Blimp (a story which is deservedly told in full later). Cartoonists themselves point to the volume of mail a particular cartoon will inspire – but as a working journalist I have learned to be wary of the contents of my mailbox, at least as an honest representation of *vox populi*.

My hunch is that cartoonists have their greatest influence when they encapsulate the existing mood of their audience, rather than when they try to create one. During the two world wars, cartoonists of all political shades happily volunteered for the artistic war effort, along the predictable lines of 'Britain can take it' or 'The Germans are beastly' or 'We (the British) are the good guys'. We probably were the good guys, but the fact remains that almost invariably, the cartoonists reflected the tide of current opinion; they did not inspire it. This is why Bruce Bairnsfather, with his realistic images of life in the trenches of the First World War, is so important. As far as his hero, Old Bill, was concerned, the enemy was the British Army and its officers, rather than the poor bloody Hun who was living in just as wet and nasty a trench on the other side of the barbed wire. So it was the troops, not the Home Front, who hailed his work. Cartoons themselves rarely enter the front line of politics. The only cartoon of recent years that I can recall seeing in a political demonstration was a poisonous effort produced by the National Front for their anti-immigration marches in 1974. It showed a villainous black man beating an old white lady, and it had been enlarged to be reproduced on banners held by the marchers. The police, to their credit, insisted that the black face be covered over before allowing the march to proceed.

It is, I suppose, a tribute to the level-headedness of voters that they tend to remain unmoved by passionate campaigns in the media, whether by cartoonists or writers, to sway the nation's opinions. All of the efforts of the Beaverbrook chain of newspapers, for instance, were unable to build a national consensus against the Common Market and the *Daily Mail*'s spurt of enthusiasm for Sir Oswald Mosley's British Union of Fascists in 1934 had little lasting impact.

There are times when this can change. During the long years of exile spent by Helen Vlachos, the Greek newspaperwoman who opposed the military junta, she stressed the importance of the cartoonist in maintaining some kind of opposition; even under a controlled press. The printed word, she argued, was too precise. A critic of the colonels could be silenced. But cartoonists, whose attacks could be ambiguous, had more leeway. Greek cartoonists began to draw a disproportionate number of scenes based on Spanish politics under the ageing General Franco, attacking Fascism as the political perversion of tired old men. Greek readers got the point that Spain was being used as a parallel for Greece, while the censors found themselves with little cause to complain. But, again, the cartoonists were building upon a foundation of Greek opposition to the junta which had already been laid. The cartoonists provided a rallying point for the Opposition – but the cartoonists had not called them to arms.[7]

Of course, there is no law which says that cartoonists must be controversial. The grand old man of *Punch*, Tenniel, and his successors Sir Bernard Partridge, Raven Hill and Ernest Shepherd, chose to attack safe targets, like Bolshevism, usually portrayed as a foul and dirty nihilist, often equipped with a bomb. It would be easy to classify all cartoonists and to say that the *Punch* men were conservative, and that Low, Carruthers Gould, Gerald Scarfe and Ralph Steadman were radical. But this would be a mistake. The fact is that a hearteningly high proportion of cartoonists whose politics are blatantly conservative show a healthy lack of respect for the politicians of all parties. Cummings of the *Express*, or JAK of the *Evening Standard* take a clear delight in hurling pictorial abuse at their political allies. The real distinction between cartoonists is not one of political belief, but one of style. Style is an elusive quality to pin down, but compare the fussy, line-filled drawings of Tenniel or Partridge with the clear outlines of Low's cartoons or the economy of line in Phil Evans's work and it is clear that we are looking at different generations, different techniques. Part of the explanation lies in the demands of modern mass production. Low's own autobiography suggests that the poor quality of printing paper in Australia and New Zealand, making it difficult to reproduce fine lines and detail, helps to account for the bold, confident styles of the artists who began their careers there.[8] But there is another explanation for this difference in the artists' approach. The *Punch* school tended to be reflective, more concerned with the pictorial product than thudding home any weighty political message. This concern for what the cartoon *shows*, rather than what it *says*, is in direct contrast to the aggressive, committed art of a Dyson or a Low.

It would be tempting to attribute this difference of approach to the passing years, and say that Low was direct and modern, and that Tenniel and his disciples were old-fashioned and staid. But since some modes in the art of the newspaper cartoon show continuation of style from generation to generation, this is not strictly true. Turn from the busy works of the Strube of the 1930s, his faithful characters and their healthy mistrust of their political leaders, to the Giles cartoons of the 1960s. The parallel between the two artists leaps into life. And Dyson and Low were contemporaries of Bernard Partridge, their cartoons jostling on the same news-stands and commenting on the same events, although their vision seems centuries apart. Low, Partridge and Raven Hill met one night for dinner, and exchanged views about their varying styles. Low later recalled, 'We disagreed frequently and emphatically, we each consumed two helpings of roast duck and we parted friends'.[9]

Stylistic distinctions are unreliable and readers should make up their own minds. But I think I discern three quite clear and distinct traditions in the British political cartoon; each tradition happily enfolding left-and right-wingers without a temporal progression. The grand tradition is that of the classicists, best seen in the pages of *Punch*. (In the last century, *Punch* had a reputation similar to that of *Private Eye* in our own day; but these things change.) The statesmen are huge figures, dominating the page. Their features are nobly set; they adopt the heroic aspects of Greek statues; they are stern, just and wise. The cartoons seem almost to have been stamped with some official seal, as suitable for great and stirring occasions. They are at their best when depicting scenes like the death of monarchs, with wreaths being laid and ranks of soldiers with bowed heads. It is easy to understand why Sir John Tenniel fell so easily into the style; he was brought to the pages of *Punch* after his noble and uplifting frescoes for the new House of Commons had been widely admired. The Partridges and Shepherds and Illingworths followed in his solemn footsteps. It is charitable to recall that when Tenniel began, there were no press photographs, so he was an illustrator of current affairs as well as a cartoonist in the modern sense.

But Will Dyson, one of the angriest and most ferocious cartoonists ever to sketch a line, also drew upon this tradition. Dyson, like so many of the best British cartoonists like Low, Gibbard, Rigby and Waite, came from 'down under'. Whether it was the sense of exile from their Australian and New Zealand homes, or the reaction at finding the closed, class-conscious society of England, which led them to be so direct and bold in their work is uncertain. But Dyson was an ideologue. He began as an uncompromising socialist, with little faith in the reformist ambitions of the Labour Party, and great hatred and contempt for the British ruling class. Later in life, he followed the obscure theology of Social Credit.

'Humour and good humour are virtues in the private sphere', he once said. 'But elsewhere they are a cowardice and a thinness of the blood.'[10] And yet Dyson, in his draughtsmanship, was a classicist. The huge noble figures of workers, or the equally huge (but clearly evil) politicians, businessmen and generals dominated the front pages of the *Daily Herald* in the turbulent, strike and strife-torn years before the First World War. The clean, brawny arms of his workers were set in counterpoint to the fat, gross or demonic rulers. Dyson's was a Manichean universe, divided between absolute good and absolute evil.

During the First World War, Dyson's anti-Kaiser cartoons were so forceful (and so useful for the British propaganda industry) that he almost became acceptable to his hated British Establishment. In 1916, they even gave him a cartoon exhibition at the Savoy Hotel. He became an official war artist, and some of the captions to his brilliant sketches of the Western Front reveal the classic tradition in which he thought and drew. Describing soldiers in the trenches, he wrote: 'They come out of endless holes and go into endless holes like lonely ants bent on some ant-like service . . . Ant-like in the distance, they loom upon a nearer vision of things elemental and Homeric, big with destiny.'[11]

There was another tradition behind Dyson's work, a tradition which was strong before the First World War and which is strong once more today, although it disappeared almost entirely from British cartoons between 1918 and the 1960s. It has never been healthier than it is today, with the cruel pens of Gerald Scarfe and Ralph Steadman. The only word to describe this style is the grotesque. We can trace it back through the savage work of Daumier, through the black paintings of Goya and the sketches he made during the Spanish campaigns of the Napoleonic Wars. There were British cartoons of the same period, many of them distributed into Europe as propaganda, which showed Napoleon's face made up of dozens of mutilated corpses, weeping widows, sad orphans and dying men.

Dyson used these grotesque techniques when drawing the cold and arrogant faces of his capitalists, and his brutish Huns of the Great War. Scarfe and Steadman used the style to give us their insight of the poisoned soul of President Nixon, long before the journalists of the written word came to topple him. It is remarkable that other great cartoonists could not bring themselves to this style, no matter what the provocation. Vicky, for example, his heart rent by what he saw as the great moral cause of nuclear disarmament, was never grotesque. Even in the last agonized weeks before he died, disillusioned to the point of despair by the failure of Harold Wilson's Labour Government, his style remained formal. There was moral outrage, moral courage and devastating wit, but Vicky was never merciless. Perhaps he was too nice a man ever to hate. And I clearly remember that no matter how many times Vicky addressed himself to the shameful way in which Harold Wilson's Government refused to offend the US about the Vietnam war, he never had the well-aimed impact of the Scarfe cartoon which showed a lip-smacking Harold Wilson about to kiss the arse of Lyndon Johnson.

Until the 1960s, it was war which provoked cartoonists to adopt the grotesque mode. For Dyson the furies of class war in Edwardian Britain, or of the Second World War in the trenches were the inspiration. For the Dutch cartoonist Louis Raemaekers, raised and flowering in the classic tradition, the Great War was the catalyst which produced one of the most skilful of the cartoon propagandists. Raemaekers even boasted of his own influence in his cartoons, drawing pig-like German soldiers searching the trains from neutral Holland to stop his work crossing the border. The British Prime Minister Asquith, writing an introduction to a collection of Raemaekers' work which was heavily subsidized by Britain for export to the US, insisted that Raemaekers was 'a neutral observer'. But the force of Raemaekers, the subtlety of that not-quite-grin on the leering face of the Kaiser in the 'Zeppelin raider' cartoon, the huddled mass of Teuton evil around the corpse of Nurse Cavell, his cartoon of the sinking of the *Lusitania* – these were works which swayed men's minds.

It would need a historian, a psychologist and a social scientist to account for the revival of the grotesque spirit in the 1960s, and to account for the lack of it during the Second World War, when the German adversary was plainly very much more evil than the Kaiser. There were dozens of predictable cartoons of whole armies of skeletons, heaps of dead and refugees around the jackboots of Hitler, but few that even strove to achieve the passion of Raemaekers, or to portray the vicarious outrage of Scarfe and Steadman over Vietnam or Rhodesia. Perhaps the evil of Hitler was too total for satire, perhaps cartoonists still cherished the high hopes of international goodwill that had launched and sustained the League of Nations. Whatever the cause, the nearest we come to the grotesque between the wars lies in the anti-Jewish filth of the British Union of Fascists' magazine, the *Blackshirt*. They barely deserve the name cartoons, being simple, vicious caricatures of men with large noses.

But there is something slightly disturbing about our modern grotesques – a hint that the style itself is of more importance than its target. Every one of Scarfe's targets appears to be warped in the same way. There is little distinction of the degree of moral evil his targets are supposed to represent. It may be that Scarfe sees them all as being as bad as each other – Wilson, LBJ, Iam Smith, Denis Healey, Mrs Thatcher. But if this is so, is Scarfe trying to tell us that all public figures are a scurvy crew – without exception?

Steadman raises similar problems. It seems that he too brings the same hatred, the same vicious vision to them all. Is this real vitriol, or is there something of the mercenary about it – a kind of purchased passion? Scarfe and Steadman could properly point back to the great French grotesque artist Daumier, and the way he never lets us forget the brute in man, the foulness in politics, the law and the game of nations. And Scarfe could simply point to one of his cleverest works – a cartoon that looks like Wilson and then turn it upside down and it looks like Ted Heath. Scarfe is saying more than simply 'A plague on both your political houses'; he is saying 'A plague on all politics – and on you, the voters too'. Scarfe does have a defence against the charge that he barely bothers to distinguish between his cartoon hatreds – but it is a defence purchased at the price of the influence he can hope to exert upon us. Rather like the boy who cried 'Wolf' too often, we tend to run to Scarfe not for a particular insight into an event or a personality, but to see what caricatured horror he has conjured from this week's face. In this context, it is significant that Steadman is now better known as an illustrator, particularly of Hunter Thompson's biting satires on American life and politics, than as a cartoonist in the traditional sense.

The third of the great traditions, and almost certainly the most familiar, is one we can term the Populist. Artistically, we can trace its history back to the work of Pieter Breughel, with his teeming, crowded canvases of tiny people, scurrying about and being dominated by some great and fateful event. It is a style eminently suited to what the American New Deal politicians liked to call 'the age of the common man'. Little people, ordinary people, dwarfed by the scale of grand, historic destiny. Whether the bemused, pathetic politicians that Low drew so well, or Giles' ordinary English family with mischievous kids and the immortal Grandma, they are drawn without the awe of the classicists, and without the cruelty of the grotesques. Underlying the work of the Populists is the glum but comforting thought that we are all in the same boat, that we are all likely to make mistakes, that almost everybody is 'Us' and that there are very few of 'Them'; it is the very essence of cartoon democracy.

To ram home the point, the Populist cartoonists usually invented a regular character. Low had himself a timid-looking man with a little moustache (and sometimes a beard, until it made him too recognizable in the street), and a blandly pretty lady whom he called Joan Bull. Percy Fearson (the Poy of the *Evening News* and *Daily Mail*) had his archetypal tax-payer hounded and bemused by Dilly and Dally, the two civil servants, by Cuthbert the Whitehall rabbit, by rising prices and taxes and every other horror known to modern man. Cummings in today's *Sunday Express* has much the same harassed figure, hatless today and neatly dressed in a dark suit, but equally at the mercy of taxman, government and malign fate. Low's great rival between the wars, Sydney 'George' Strube of the *Daily Express*, created John Citizen, a sharp-eyed alert little fellow who slowly aged with his creator. John Citizen grew a moustache, and it got whiter with the years, but he always wore the same bowler hat, was always patriotic and his motto was 'Business as Usual', particularly during the Blitz.

This theme of the archetypal, down-trodden citizen has been taken to lyric heights by Frank Dickens, creator of the Bristow comic strip in today's *Evening Standard*. Bristow works in a huge, modern office block. The highlights of his life are the company newsletter, the visits of the tea-lady and a bird who visits his window ledge. His superiors are always vain and stupid, and Bristow's response is a kind of bureaucratic guerrilla warfare, blending dumb insolence with carefully-aimed incompetence in the interest not just of survival, but of survival with pride. Bristow is fat, bald, with a walrus moustache and a formal suit – somehow these attributes have continued to embody the stock British cartoon citizen since Strube's day. There are parallels to be drawn between Strube's gardener after the air raid with his insouciant defiance of Hitler's bombs, and Bristow's defiance of his company. Both are seen as representative individuals taking up arms against huge, impersonal forces, and it is in their defiance, in their bloody-mindedness that their victory lies.

Accompanying the dominance of the Populist cartoon was the growth of the State, taking an ever-larger proportion of the average voter's income and exercising authority over more and more of his affairs. Readers identified with the portrait of themselves as victims. Ironically, the growth of the State, and the growth of the mass media which accompanied the phenomenon, made for an ever-larger audience for the cartoonists. The circulation figures of British newspapers rose throughout the century until the 1960s, when television began to overwhelm the press as the dominant medium. In 1963, a brief and unsuccessful experiment in bringing cartoons to TV was tried on the popular satirical programme, 'That Was the Week That Was'. The young Timothy Birdsall, who drew the decadence of the last years of the Macmillan era, with its spy scandals, its crooked landlords and speculators and its call-girls, was hired to draw instant cartoons on the programme. The experiment did not survive Birdsall's tragic early death from leukaemia.[12] By this time, the cartoon and the comic had themselves become well-enough established to inspire the experimental artists of the 1960s.

But some things stayed the same. The doves of Peace, the dark-cloaked skeletons of Death, the flat-capped queues of the unemployed; these perennial cartoon symbols, a kind of artistic shorthand, became basic building blocks of the trade. Even David Low, who tried hard not to get stuck by out-dated symbols, found that when he tried to modernize John Bull by changing his sex and reducing Bull's traditionally vast waistline, he had simply created a new cliché, near enough to the original to be always recognizable, and with anonymous enough features to become a cartoonist's stock-in-trade young woman. There had been some competition, when young women got the vote for the 1929 election, to see whose version of the 'New Woman' would become dominant. The old types had to be jettisoned – Dyson's wickedly elegant hostesses, *Punch*'s noble-browed and virtuous maidens, and its broad-bottomed peasant matrons. The face of Low's Joan became the new norm, still recognizable today in the Gambols' comic strip.

And now Low's new woman herself has been outmoded, perhaps most characteristically by John Kent's Varoomshka, a deliciously long-thighed lovely with sultry eyes – a perfect Britannia for the years after Swinging London. Varoomshka is the *Candide* of cartoons, eternally innocent, asking simple questions from the politicians of the day and receiving embarrassingly honest answers. Varoomshka is important because it is through her that some of the most telling, bitter charges against our politicians are levelled. The cartoon is based on an assumption of hypocrisy and self-interest in our political leaders, upon John Kent's clear declaration of war upon the statesman breed. The style of the strip cartoon is highly flexible – there is frame enough for dialogue (and even dialectic) to take place between the characters, and for their faces to go through several expressions and moods. As a result, Kent has been able to experiment with a number of different techniques, of which the most successful has been the blending of two stock images, Harold Wilson and Idi Amin. The result may look like a fat Wilson in black-face, a kind of political Al Jolson, but it gives a richness of characterization that single-frame cartoon often lacks. But this too depends upon

Kent's fundamental assumption, that today's audience is mature enough to accept abuse in their cartoons as well as wit. Not all of Kent's targets are so complaisant; trade union leader Jack Jones was moved to bring libel proceedings against one Varoomshka jibe.

Cartoonists depend upon symbols. They need uniformly recognizable types, so that a social context can be suggested without a lengthy, accompanying text. Rich men are easy – a top hat, or even a fat cigar will do. Shop-floor workers can be identified by a flat cap or overalls. Countries have human symbols, like Uncle Sam, or France's Marianne, or John Bull. In the first half of the century, it was still possible to show Britain by a lion (or in the Second World War by a bulldog), France by a cockerel, Germany by an eagle or by a dachshund (depending on the state of Anglo–German relations). But with the 1930s and the coming of the dictators, the national ruler took over from the national symbol as the identifying mark. One of the last appearances of the Russian bear, sitting in a jeep beside an Atom bomb at a Victory parade, came predictably in *Punch*, from the pen of Illingworth in 1946. And even then, the bear looked remarkably like Stalin. The John Bull figure is now largely restricted to foreign cartoonists, and British readers see the nation symbolized in the familiar features of a Harold Wilson, an Edward Heath or a Jim Callaghan.

They are none the less recognizable for that. A politician can be said to have reached maturity when all the major cartoonists can draw him from memory. It is an odd process, the way the cartoonists' guild goes about developing the definitive portrait. One of the most difficult tasks in recent years was to get a universally-acceptable cartoon of Selwyn Lloyd, a senior Tory Minister and later Speaker of the House of Commons. He had a bland face, and occasionally (but not always) wore spectacles. He had a small, unobtrusive nose, an unremarkable mouth, an ordinary chin. Everybody agreed that he was quite short, which was a help, and he had a jaunty air. The pages of the British press were thick with unidentifiable but jaunty midgets. Then Vicky invented a new nose for Selwyn Lloyd; under which Lloyd appeared properly dwarfish. Selwyn Lloyd was henceforth known among British cartoonists for his nose, though it bore little resemblance to the original.[13]

But on the whole, British politicians have been kind to cartoonists. Lloyd George's flowing white hair, Churchill's jowls and cigar, Macmillan's droopy eyebrows, the teeth of Edward Heath – they were all gifts to the artists. And when they were facially unremarkable, like Harold Wilson, they provided a pipe and a certain kind of raincoat to fix the image. Cummings once drew a wholly recognizable Harold Wilson without drawing the eyes, nose or mouth. Jensen of the *Sunday Telegraph* made Wilson's tartan-lined raincoat into a comic-strip hero by having Wilson walk past a newspaper stand proclaiming a Scottish Nationalist success in a by-election. Wilson took one look at the headline, removed his raincoat, turned it inside out, and a tartan-clad Wilson walked on down the street.

Kruschev's bald head, John Kennedy's hair, de Gaulle's nose and Jimmy Carter's teeth all became international currency through the cartoonists' bush telegraph. And yet these tricks of the trade, vital though they may be, can be dangerous. Indians in British cartoons are identified by turbans, or loincloths or beds of nails. Irishmen tend to be broad-shouldered navvies wearing donkey jackets emblazoned with the name of a building firm, or trench-coated thugs with low foreheads and blunt jaws. Such images may be useful, and they may be innocently drawn. But simply because such stereotypes become universally understood, they are drawn upon again and again, reinforcing prejudice and undermining trust.[14]

The fact is that cartoonists' symbols develop a life of their own. When Low invented Colonel Blimp (after many days pondering Bishop Blimp, Doctor Blimp and even Lord Blimp), he little realized how the figure would come to haunt him. The Conservative Party, suspecting that they were the real target of Low's figure, held a special exhibition to show that they were not Blimp. Two obscure Colonels threatened to sue Low for libel. One Australian claimed to have been to school with Blimp.

During the Second World War a film was made about Colonel Blimp, and a major national debate began about the desirability of allowing foreigners (particularly the Americans) to see this well-meaning, but indefatigably stupid example of the British officer corps. Churchill himself went to the première (taking Anthony Eden) and immediately agreed with the headline in that morning's *Daily Mail* 'Blimp film must NOT go abroad'. A Whitehall committee was formed to give a formal opinion. It decided that the film should stay in Britain for the benefit of the British Army's reputation. Some months later, when the film finally reached New York, all the advertising featured Blimp as a randy old lecher (the original Blimp thought sex was something that came between five and seven). In Russia, the Blimp figure was borrowed by Low's old friend and fellow cartoonist Boris Efimov as the kind of capitalist chap who was stopping Britain from launching an immediate invasion of occupied Europe.[15]

The odd thing about Blimp is that he was unnecessary. Blimp was simply a fat figure with a long white moustache, and was usually to be found in a Turkish bath, whose statements were adequately humorous one-line jokes in themselves. ('How can we expect Mussolini to behave decently if we object to his dropping gas bombs?' . . . or 'Gad sir, Hitler was right. We should absorb our unemployed by starting them building concentration camps to lock themselves in' . . . or 'There must be no monkeying with the liberty of Indians to do what they are damn well told.' My own favourite is: 'Before we can allow Russia to protect the British Empire we must insist on her restoring the capitalist system.') These alone were funny enough. But like Andy Capp, or Charles Schulz's Peanuts with Charley Brown (who became the subject of a hit record) the visual image combined with the jokes and the attitudes to invade and conquer a national, even international, consciousness. They provide almost terrifying examples of the power of the media to create myths, and of our own frightening readiness to accept them.

One day, doubtless, a sufficient battery of experts and computers and guinea pigs will be assembled to allow us to understand this process: how it is that myths are made. For the moment, we had better accept that it all has something to do with the combination of words and pictures; that the total effect of a cartoon is equal to very much more than the sum of its parts. A similar kind of process took place with the international popularity of the James Bond films, and perhaps with certain TV series like Kojak. They are all characters with whom we have grown familiar, and their deeds do not surprise us. No matter what happens to them, no matter what international crisis provokes Colonel Blimp, or Strube's John Citizen, or John Kent's Varoomshka, their reaction will be predictable. They represent a fixed and faithful point in a changing world, and evidently we need them.

There is a Giles cartoon of 1955 which shows how we need cartoons in a slightly different way. The day shift is leaving the factory, and among them is a robot, cycling away from the gates with the human workers, and clearly chatting up a pretty girl as she too cycles home. One of the human workers angrily follows, muttering that it is one thing when the robot takes his job, but he's damned if he will let a hunk of metal pinch his girlfriend. It is a comforting cartoon. We all have a fear of automation, of unemployment, but the fear can be neutralized – robots and girls don't mix. Or maybe they will one day and the cartoon is subtler than I thought. One of the reasons I chose to include this cartoon, even though it is not strictly political, is to compare it with another cartoon, from *Punch* of 1933, which shows a robot as a clear menace to men and to jobs. It may be a changing world, in which some cartoon themes and characters can give us a comforting illusion of stability, but many of the great causes which excited cartoonists of Edwardian days are alive and potent subjects still.

The cartoons in this selection provide a brisk little social history of their own. They show how fashions change, how the faces of the great men change, how the frontiers of nations are endlessly altered, and how the backgrounds and details which give the drawings their authentic period flavour shift and flow as though each decade provided a new environment of its own. The way we are taught history in our schools reinforces this idea of constant change. We know of the Edwardian era, which stopped in 1914 and was replaced by the Great War. And then came the twenties with the Charleston and the General Strike and air travel and the Great Depression and unemployment. And then that ended with Hitler and the unemployed got jobs in the re-armament factories and we moved into the next new period of the Second World War, to be followed by the 1945 Labour Government and austerity. And then came Suez and Harold Macmillan and Ban the Bomb and the Profumo scandal, which brought us Harold Wilson's Government, and God help us, here we are again already. We are accustomed to seeing history as a series of landmarks, each leading to a new direction, as though life changed with the fall of Governments and the shortening of women's skirts.

But it wasn't really like that. The environment changes much faster than the people. One of the earliest cartoons in this book mocks the surprise of politicians during the Boer War at the readiness and willingness of the Boers to fight. There are any number of American cartoons of the 1960s which make the same point about Vietnam, and near the end of this book is a Trog cartoon about Northern Ireland which points to a similar moral. Will Dyson's cartoons about class hatred in 1913 has parallels from almost every decade of this century. And the anti-Bolshevik cartoons which *Punch* published endlessly in the 1920s could be reprinted in some daily papers today. The Labour Party as a tool of Moscow; the Conservatives as the tool of big business; the workers must accept lower wages; our export salesmen must do better.

There is a marvellous Raven Hill cartoon of 1931 when the pound sterling itself, hero-villain of so many of today's headlines, is the cartoon's main character, delicately trying to balance on a tightrope before the eyes of the world. All through the century, the cartoonists reflect the common preoccupations of the common man; budgets, strikes, defence, unemployment, Northern Ireland, arms races and so on. It is almost as though nothing fundamental ever changes, and in at least one important sense, Britain has stayed the same. The Empire may have gone, alliances may have changed, the predominant industries may have changed places, but Britain is still recognizably the same kind of industrial society that we were in 1900. We still have workers, seeking the best possible wage; we still have owners and managers, seeking to sell at a profit, and we still have a mass market of consumers, hunting the lowest possible price. We must still export to buy that half of our food which we do not grow. The patterns of production, manpower and consumption may all have evolved in degree, but not in kind, over the last seventy-seven years and the cartoons in this book illustrate that.

These cartoons are accessible in a way that the famous works of Cruikshank and Gillray in the days of Napoleon are not. All of the events which inspired them took place within the living memory of some of us. And the works of the Gillrays, the Cruikshanks, the Rowlandsons and the Sayers deal with a society which was differently composed. The landed interest, the aristocracy and the owners of the great estates had a political importance which they had lost by 1900. In those days, the Monarchy was without doubt the most regular target and topic of the cartoonists. In this century, it has figured as a theme a bare handful of times – the Abdication of Edward VIII, the marriages of Princes and Princesses lead to the occasional cartoon, but partly because of convention (and Low complained that no national paper of the 1930s could be persuaded to print his caricature of the Monarchy)[16] and mainly because the Monarchy is no longer in the political arena, the subject has been dropped. Even some of the cartoonists' conventions are gone – the only person these days who is ever cartooned as falling off a horse is Princess Anne, which brings two anachronisms together. Most sadly, the vicious energy, the sheer violence of political hatred which were the essence of Gillray and Cruikshank, has long since ceased to be the dominant style. Dyson had it, Scarfe and Steadman have touched it, but the constant, merciless screech of the Regency cartoonists has settled in the twentieth century to a well-mannered murmur.

We, as an audience, probably deserve a much quieter life, although I doubt whether our politicians should get off as lightly as they do. There are many reasons for this softer tone, including the simple fact that most modern cartoonists need to produce a new cartoon, a new idea each day. I cannot explain how they dredge their imaginations to do it – I can only admire their energy. And then there is the sheer richness of different styles. In Gillray's day there was one dominant style – to fix your target on a pin, chain him down, and then cudgel him below the belt as hard and as often as possible. It made for bold and memorable cartoons, and for interesting risks in a political career, but it lacked variety. And cartoonists in Gillray's day had but one market – a tiny élite of literate and politically-informed people, most of them in London. Cartoonists today tend to work for one main newspaper, with a clearly-defined readership and a clearly-defined political line. There is not the cut-throat competition for one tiny market which sharpened Gillray's pen. And there is something else, very much more subtle, which has blunted many of the pens of our own day. It is a kind of smugness about Britain, perhaps an inheritance from the war, when cartoonists like Low and Strube were in the front line of the propaganda battle for the Home Front.[17] Cartoonists learned (and were expected) to celebrate and to promote some of our comforting British myths about ourselves.

There is a cartoon by Strube about the Blitz, showing John Citizen coming out of his shelter after an air raid, and his wife calls up to ask if everything is all right. John Citizen, concerned only for the safety of his prize vegetable marrow, shouts down that it hasn't suffered a scratch. Now that's the spirit! Hitler can't worry us, we're a nation of gardeners.

Some thirty years later, during the wave of bombs in London placed by the Angry Brigade and the IRA, the home of the Tory Cabinet Minister Robert Carr was badly damaged by a bomb. JAK's cartoon in the *Evening Standard*, which I think of as one of his finest, showed an angry deputation of neighbours on Carr's demolished doorstep, demanding that he hold quieter parties in future.

I think there is a parallel between those cartoons, a myth (which may well be true) that they share. It is a clever way of portraying a stiff upper lip, that grand old British virtue. JAK's was a very funny cartoon, and if it stopped one Londoner from panicking at the thought of a bomb wave in the city then JAK deserves a pension. But are we British really like that, or is it simply that we are so accustomed to the myth that we are all supposed to have a stiff upper lip that we would die of shame if we showed any sign of fear or human panic on such occasions?

Tentatively, I put forward the proposition that the experience of two world wars and one unending Cold War (for all three of which there was a broad national consensus of support) has been to mobilize many of our cartoonists into the job of being custodians of our national myth. Any cartoon of the Giles family on a foreign holiday illustrates my argument. Foreign men pinch female British bottoms, and foreign birds make eyes at Father, who has tummy trouble. Foreign traffic police are a modern Gestapo, and foreign grub is worse. Grandma misses her glass of milk stout. It's a dangerous place, Abroad.

This phenomenon, predictably, is most marked in the *Daily Express* and the *Evening Standard*, both Beaverbrook newspapers. But you can also see it in the *Daily Mail*, in the old cartoons of Illingworth, or the more recent work of Emmwood. There is a hint of this, although not its xenophobic aspect, in David Low's TUC carthorse, that dear old, strong old bumbling thing, whom I always associate with George Orwell's horse, Boxer, in *Animal Farm*. It seems to be saying that the TUC is the British workman at heart: slow-witted, stolid but sound and as patriotic as hell. It is a very gentle way of delivering a potent and perhaps subliminal political message.

I am probably attributing to some very fine cartoonists deep and dark motives which may never have entered their heads. This is not what I want to do. Cartoons, being complex blends of information, work upon us in complex ways. Cartoons are important to newspapers; they can be important to governments as propaganda. They have dramatic political effect – as Low knew well from the time when Lord Halifax, the Foreign Minister, called Low in to say that it would be easier to keep the peace with the Dictators if Low eased off his attacks on Hitler and Mussolini.[18]

Cartoons can be subversive, just as they can help to reinforce and justify the status quo. Dyson was more than subversive; he was a rallying cry to class war. But Vicky was a gentle subversive, and so, in the context of the 1930s, was Low. In the 1950s, Low buckled down and became an unwilling Cold Warrior. No, that is unfair. He accepted that a state of Cold War existed, and for very good and persuasive reasons he chose to support our side. His 1951 cartoon, 'What a headache sometimes to be with America – but to be without it, O Lor!', with the alternative pictured as an evil Stalin with a sinister big sack, shows what I mean.

Perhaps the most subversive cartoon I know is by the American comic-strip artist R. Crumb. It shows a devastated urban wasteland, a city levelled to the ground by a nuclear blast or urban warfare or some nameless horror. In it stands one figure, a neatly-dressed middle-American citizen, carrying a TV set and looking helplessly for somewhere to plug it in. It is an image of Western industrial society in our time that worries me more than any other. That is my problem; doubtless you have yours.

Martin Walker

REFERENCES

1. Professor Gombrich's definition was read to an audience at the University of Kent on October 31, 1975, at the formal opening of the Centre for the Study of Cartoons and Caricature.

2. David Low. *British Cartoonists*. Collins 1942. p 21.

3. *Punch*, March 4, 1914. A special supplement to commemorate Tenniel's career. Balfour's comment was made at a dinner given to Tenniel on the occasion of his retirement in 1901, and is quoted in the *Punch* supplement.

4. Quoted by Carruthers Gould's grand-daughter, Anne Gould, in 'The picture-politics of FCG', *20th Century Studies*, December 1975.

5. Arthur Christiansen *Headlines all my life*. Heinemann 1961. p 91.

6. A. J. P. Taylor *Beaverbrook*. Hamish Hamilton 1972. p 434.

7. Helen Vlachos's remarks were made in a public lecture, and are quoted in Fritz Behrendt's 'The freedom of the political cartoonist', *20th Century Studies*, December 1975.

8. For Low's difficulties in persuading the London *Star* to give him adequate space for his bold cartoons, see Low's autobiography, Michael Joseph 1956, pp 86–8.

9. A marvellous account of Low's meeting with the *Punch* classicists can be found on pp 208–12 of Low, *op cit*.

10. Quoted in John Jensen's 'Curious – I seem to hear a child weeping', a profound and sensitive study of one cartoonist by another, *20th Century Studies*, December 1975.

11. Jensen's essay. *op cit*.

12. A similar experiment was launched in 1976 by Granada TV, with the *Guardian*'s cartoonist Les Gibbard.

13. The source for this story, like so much that we know about Vicky, was his close friend and fellow-giant in British journalism, James Cameron.

14. For an incisive analysis of this (and most other aspects of the cartoonist's work), see Colin Seymour-Ure's brilliant essay 'How Special Are Cartoonists?', *20th Century Studies*. December 1975.

15. Low's autobiography, *op cit*. pp 264–76.

16. David Low 'Ye Madde Designer'. *The Studio* 1935, p 41.

17. Low's own account of his brief and unsatisfactory efforts on behalf of the Ministry of Information is told in his autobiography, *op cit*. pp 322–3.

18. Low's autobiography, *op cit*. p 278.

FRANCIS CARRUTHERS GOULD

The Westminster Gazette   January 23, 1900

In a staunchly Liberal paper, Carruthers Gould was a staunchly Liberal cartoonist, the first ever to be hired on to the staff of a British daily. No great artist, he became famous for the intimacy of his political knowledge, and later, for his determined hounding of the Conservative Joseph Chamberlain.

The opening of the Boer War brought a series of shocks for the ill-equipped and badly trained British Army. In a progression of military disasters, the Boer superiority in marksmanship, mobility and weapons was cruelly rammed home. The Liberal Opposition, uncertain of the War's wisdom, were quick to make political capital from the early reverses – and the Government was equally quick to charge the Liberals with lack of patriotism.

SUCH A SURPRISE!

MR BALFOUR: *Fancy, Ridley! they've actually got horses!*
SIR M. W. RIDLEY: *And look, Arthur, they've got rifles too! What a shame to deceive us!*

SIR JOHN TENNIEL

Punch March 7, 1900

One of Tenniel's last cartoons, and in the classic mould. The early reverses of the ill-led British troops in the Boer War led the European press (which had no love for wave-ruling, Empire-grabbing Britain) to suggest that the Boers might win. But the lion comes roaring out of his lair as reinforcements are rushed to the Cape, and the energies of Empire begin to mobilize. The European asses scurry away. The king of beasts rules, OK.

Who said '*Dead*'?

J. M. STANNIFORTH

The Western Mail, Cardiff June 9, 1900

Stout John Bull, armed with a stick, has soundly thrashed the weeping Boer (armed with a rifle). In fact, at this stage of the South African War, the tiny Boer Republics of the Transvaal and Orange Free State were far from beaten, and their eventual subjugation was to require the mobilization of the Empire's military forces, the introduction of concentration camps and some £217 million.

The outbreak of the Boxer rebellion in China, against all the occupying powers of Europe, was an object lesson to British strategists in just how thinly-spread were the Empire's troops, particularly when an isolated Britain faced a hostile, pro–Boer Europe.

In international and domestic unpopularity, the Boer War has parallels with America's difficulties in Vietnam. Britain drew the lesson and began to forge a series of military alliances, with Japan, and later with France and Russia.

ANOTHER ON THE LIST

JOHN BULL: '*Hello, there's John Chinaman asking for a thrashing now! Well, if he will persist, he must have it!*'

FRANCIS CARRUTHERS GOULD

The Westminster Gazette   October 11, 1900

The general election, held while the war raged, was known as the Khaki election, and it was marked by violent scenes and unusual bitterness between 'loyal' Conservatives and 'disloyal' Liberals. Lloyd George had to be smuggled from one turbulent meeting disguised as a policeman. Balfour gave the battered Liberals his sympathy: Joe Chamberlain, pictured creeping round the corner, is all sharp nose and monocle on the body of a dog. Chamberlain treasured his collection of Gould cartoons, but once wrote to him to ask that he 'not be pictured as a cur'.

The Bobs of the poster is John Robert, the Field Marshal, and with General Kitchener, the favourite soldier of the day.

CHRISTIAN CONSOLATION

Mr Balfour (to a defeated Liberal): *My dear sir, of course you're an 'honourable and patriotic' man; and as for those placards, how could I have supposed that they would have been taken literally?*

[*See Mr Balfour's speech at Bingley on Tuesday.*]

FRANCIS CARRUTHERS GOULD

The Westminster Gazette   May 3, 1904

The story of Brer Rabbit was at the height of its popularity in Britain when Gould began to mine it for scenes he could apply to contemporary politics; it went well with his gift for portraying politicians as animals. Here we have the unhappy alliance of Balfour's Conservative Party, and Joseph Chamberlain's Liberal Unionists, who split away from the Liberal Party because they refused to accept the Liberal policy of Home Rule for Ireland. The two-party system forced Chamberlain into the arms of the Tories but he was too progressive an industrialist, and too bold a politician, ever to be happy in this coalition. The Tories benefited; hitherto they had been the party of the landowners, and Chamberlain's supporters were middle-class industrialists. This coalition led to the modern Conservative Party, and gave it a broad enough base to compete with the growing electoral force of the working class. With hindsight, we can also see Chamberlain's switch as the death-knell of the old Liberals.

Brer Rabbit he up en say he have monstus respeck fer Brer Fox, en he hope he ain't gwineter eat him. Brer Fox 'low dat he ain't gwineter eat Brer Rabbit, but ef Brer Rabbit sass him he gwineter push him inter de water – ker-blunk!

FRANCIS CARRUTHERS GOULD

The Westminster Gazette   February 10, 1906

The growth of the Labour movement was seen by many as a fundamental threat to stability. The Liberals tended to the view that chaos would be more likely if the new working classes were excluded from the system. Accordingly, for the 1906 election, Gladstone's son arranged an electoral pact with the embryonic Labour Party, by which Liberals did not stand against Labour candidates. The result was a Labour presence in the House of Commons of more than fifty seats. Industrial strife continued, and the Liberals found themselves persuaded to pass more radical social and trade union legislation than they had intended.

This is not a cartoon in the purest sense, in spite of the presence of the grand old symbol John Bull. But the convention of making a simple political statement, by drawing two people in conversation, has become commonplace. It is interesting that Gould seems to be trying to sway doubtful Liberal supporters to his thinking, rather than his Tory enemies.

THE OLD FOGY: *Oh, Mr Bull, isn't it dreadfully revolutionary to have all these representatives of Labour in the House of Commons?*
MR BULL: *Not a bit of it. It* WOULD *be if they* WEREN'T *there.*

33

BERNARD PARTRIDGE

Punch   January 29, 1908

Partridge was. the heir to Tenniel in *Punch*'s pages, and by this time *Punch*'s cartoons carried all the authority of a statement from His Majesty's Government (or at least so one German Ambassador told Berlin). There is an elegant ambiguity about this cartoon – the attacked capitalist is not sympathetically drawn, but neither is that sly grin on Keir Hardie's face. It is not clear which side Partridge is taking. But the dog's ferocity, and its French jacobin hat (a cartoon symbol of subversive foreign ideologies since French revolutionary days) show that Partridge was worried. The *Leitmotif* of potential class war is clearly present. There is an interesting echo of a famous nineteenth-century *Punch* cartoon, featuring similar dogs, and titled 'Cry havoc, and let slip the dogs of war'. Partridge would have been familiar with it.

A WAITING GAME

LABOUR PARTY (to CAPITALIST). '*That's all right, Guv'nor. I won't let him bite you.* (side, to dog.) *Wait till you've grown a bit, my beauty, and you'll get a bigger mouthful!*'

BERNARD PARTRIDGE

Punch   March 31, 1909

One of *Punch*'s national goddesses, looking pensive rather than envious, at the height of the naval arms race between Britain's traditionally dominant fleet and the upstart naval threat of the economically-powerful German Reich. The naval rivalry probably did more to sway British public opinion against Germany (hitherto the French had been the natural enemy) than any other factor.

The British Navy, the loyalty of the Colonies, the envy of the German rival, the Empire on which the sun never sets – all the great popular myths of patriotic Britain are here brilliantly brought together.

THE CALL OF THE BLOOD

GERMANIA. '*A* dreadnought *for Britain from New Zealand? These lion-cubs are splendid! I wish I had an eaglet or two like that.*'

37

BERNARD PARTRIDGE

Punch   April 28, 1909

The Conservatives' worst fears are realized; the Liberal Party, already infected by that electoral pact with Labour which helped them win the 1906 election, introduced a budget which threatened to tax the rich to enable some little comfort in the form of minute old-age pensions and a modicum of sickness and unemployment insurance to go to the workers. Germany had enjoyed such a system for a generation, but for the British Conservatives, and in particular for the House of Lords, this budget was a socialist threat that had to be stopped. The House of Lords lost when the King threatened to swamp the Tory Lords with new Liberal peers, and Lloyd George won a radical reputation, and a degree of Labour gratitude, which was to stand him in good stead evermore. Again note Partridge's own ambiguity; the plutocrat is not drawn sympathetically, but the audience will remember that in the Jack and the Beanstalk fairy tale, the Giant was a villain.

RICH FARE

The Giant Lloyd-Gorgibuster:
'Fee, Fi, Fo, Fat,
I smell the blood of a plutocrat;
Be he alive or be he dead,
I'll grind his bones to make my bread.'

BERNARD PARTRIDGE

Punch   February 28, 1912

Partridge is being ambiguous again, with his unlovely coal merchant and the noble, pipe-smoking miner (in these times, a pipe was almost a cartoon symbol for integrity – a detail of which later politicians were quick to take advantage). One could see this as one of the first signs of the long love affair British public opinion has had with the miner, sympathizing with his uniquely dangerous work. Very seldom are miners portrayed as evil-minded socialists, a fact of national opinion which Edward Heath carelessly forgot in 1974. This period was perhaps the worst for British industrial relations until the General Strike, with forty-one million working days lost through strikes in 1912. It saw the growth of syndicalism, and the early negotiations of the 'Triple Alliance' of railway workers, miners and transport workers, who threatened to strike on behalf of each other's demands. The miners were by now led by men committed to a programme by which the workers would 'fight, gain control of and then administer the industry'.

.

MEAN PROFITS

COAL MERCHANT (to Miner). '*Look here, my friend, I'm against strikes, I am; but the more threats of 'em you can give me, the better it suits my book.*'

FRANK HOLLAND

John Bull. June 29, 1912

As if industrial unrest were not enough, the country's safety was also threatened by the militant suffragettes, and by the threat of civil war in Ireland. The Liberal Government depended on Irish MPs who had been elected on a Home Rule platform, for its majority. It was the Liberals' commitment to Irish Home Rule that led Chamberlain to leave the Party, and by 1912, the Government's intention to force Home Rule through Parliament had led the Protestant minority of Ulster to start arming and preparing for Civil War. Dangerously, they were supported by many officers of the British Army garrisoned in Ireland (and there were always more British troops holding down Ireland than there were in India).

John Bull magazine, 'produced for the businessman', was edited by the highly-patriotic crook Horatio Bottomley. It was something of a *Private Eye* of its day, with investigative stories, scandals and a fine cartoonist in Frank Holland, who here neatly pictures Tory confusion over Law and Order for Ulster and for the workers.

A LAW-FUL LIMERICK

FRANK HOLLAND

John Bull January 25, 1913

Ever an economic cartoonist, Holland here combines two of the major problems of the day – Irish Home Rule and the Suffragettes, whose campaign of civil disobedience to win women the vote now included setting fire to letters in pillar boxes, or pouring acid down the postal slits to ruin their contents.

Kindly Asquith proffers Home Rule to Dublin, and Carson and the House of Lords, Home Rule's implacable opponents, wait to sabotage the effort. Meanwhile, Big Ben grins (I don't know why). This theme of the lurking thug is another cartoon convention, as vital in its way as 'stage whispers' in the theatre.

BUT WILL IT REACH ITS DESTINATION?

WILL DYSON

The Daily Herald   January 8, 1913

As the strikes and industrial turbulence raged into 1913, the *Daily Herald* gave the syndicalists and the workers its support, and its brawn-iest arm was that of the radical young Australian, Will Dyson. Britain had not seen cartoons of his force and imagination since the days of Gillray and the wars against Napoleon. His weakness was that he wanted his political message to be crystal clear – hence his long cap-tions.

Dyson's main hate was the capitalist class, and though his genius and fury could hurt them, the deepest wounds were suffered by the Labour Party, then as now too timid and too law-abiding to satisfy Dyson's passions. The great exponents of Labour gradualism, Sydney and Beatrice Webb, strongly opposed Dyson.

Note the knight's quill, in place of a lance which might actually do the capitalist dragon some damage. The dragon, naturally wears a top hat. This is early Dyson, still accepting the *Punch*-based convention of classic cartoon poses, like the Knight and Maiden.

THE LADY (whom the imaginative may take to be 'Labour'): '*Alas, alas, Sir Knight, unless you slay yon Dragon, I am doomed! Since time immemorial it hath been his right to dine daily upon one maiden such as I.*'

THE DOUGHTY KNIGHT (whom one might identify with that other valiant Warrior 'The Labour Party'): '*Nay, nay, dear Lady, to slay him were a brutal and a messy work indeed, but forth shall I go, fearlessly holding him in conclave, and peradventure may persuade him to accept but half a maiden daily for his portion!*'

F. H. TOWNSEND

Punch   February 17, 1913

Perhaps you have to be a golfer to appreciate this cartoon but it expresses perfectly the smugness and complacency of *Punch* and much of British life as Europe geared up for war. Strikes, women and Irishmen raged at home. A goodly proportion of *Punch* readers were golfers, who would appreciate the joke of 'Follow the line of the S', but the real message is that the Englishman gets on with the job, and ignores the regrettable failings of others. It is a stiff-upper-lip cartoon, and it is happily drawn. The note 'Love from Ethel' is a nice touch.

Acid on the golf greens was an occasional suffragette tactic, like acid in the letter box. The British Establishment's reaction varied from a malicious hatred (force-feeding of women hunger-strikers and the use of the Cat and Mouse Act) to *Punch*-style humour. *Punch*, to its credit, even published a cartoon of squads of battered policemen, defeated by 'The Suffragette who knew Ju-jitsu'.

ACIDULATED GOLF
'Don't know how to play this, Caddie?'
'Why, you've got a grand line, Sir. Follow the S. The other gentleman's bunkered in the E.'

FRANK HOLLAND

John Bull   March 18, 1913

Again Holland gives us many themes for the price of one. 'A place in the sun' was what the German Kaiser demanded, which provoked British concern because it could mean he was after some of that Empire on which the sun never set. It was a prophetic phrase – First World War fighter pilots were to have a saying 'Watch for the Hun in the Sun'.

But it's clear that God cannot be on the German side. Even the sun looks heartbroken at the eclipse of old England. And Germany's vaunted air superiority was of little use in 1914, when the battlefronts moved too fast for the air bases to keep up. The real war in the air did not begin until 1916, by which time Britain and France were technologically abreast of the Germans, although air superiority switched back and forth between the two sides throughout the war. Significantly, air supremacy is seen here in terms of airships and Zeppelins, which the Germans later used to bomb London, to little effect.

'A PLACE IN THE SUN' –

(*The military aerial strength of Germany is supreme, being about ten times that of Great Britain.*)

– and one 'in the shade'

47

WILL DYSON

Daily Herald   April 25, 1913

This is the classic Dyson style; savage, bold blows of the pen as innocence confronts evil. The peasant's patched clothes and clogs suggest some artistic licence on Dyson's part, and notice the hint of anti-semitism in the way Dyson has drawn the features of the patriot-arms dealer. The spats and the top hat are the symbols of class hatred, the cruel frown on the face a promise of ill-will.

Dyson's fundamental message, by the way, was quite right. The arms dealers sold to all comers (see G. B. Shaw's play *Major Barbara* for a perverse justification of this), and as late as 1916, Britain was paying German manufacturers licence fees to use artillery fuses, and paying in gold through neutral Holland. The Germans did not seem to object that the fuses would kill Germans, nor did Britain object to sustaining the German war effort with gold. There was a quixotic purity about international capitalism in those days.

THE MAN BEHIND *ALL* THE GUNS

WILL DYSON

Daily Herald   June 19, 1913

Will Dyson, the Irish troubles, Law and Order and industrial unrest in the Black Country make for a potent combination, but the political message of this cartoon falls a little flat. The message was not new – Frank Holland had been making the same point in *John Bull*. But what is remarkable is the style of Dyson in this drawing, using the old convention of two men conversing. It is a remarkably recognizable Asquith (Liberal Prime Minister), but a vicious caricature all the same. That grotesque bulge of the belly, the way the chin recedes in a straight line from the nose and the nonchalance of the hands in the pockets. And all this is balanced by the dumb stupidity and awesome backside of the policeman – the effect is to make you despise Asquith and his henchman, but not to fear two creatures so ridiculous.

ASQUITH (to his sturdy henchman): '*No – don't worry too much about these Ulster Orangemen, but, of course, keep your eye on the Black Country. We have determined there shall be no bloodshed and violence tolerated in this country save that which is offered in the name of the Christian religion!*'

WILL DYSON

Daily Herald   July 2, 1914

Three days after the assassination of the Archduke Franz Ferdinand at Sarajevo, which set in motion the diplomatic panic leading up to the outbreak of war, Dyson asserts once more the threat of class war, this time on the land rather than on the shop floor. Again the device of two figures conversing, and again Dyson uses the contrast of the neat, but faintly ridiculous, uniform of the soldier, and the casually comfortable dress of the farm labourer.

The Syndicalist movement, which had hoped for great things from the Agricultural Workers' Strike (which represented a new industrial sector for them) was to be overtaken by the events that led to war.

THE AGRICULTURAL UNION

('Farmers are stopping milk from going to farm strikers' babies.' – News Item.)

SOLDIER MAN: '*Why don't 'ee join th' Army, Garge, loike I, t' foight Germans when they coom.*'

FARMER'S MAN: '*But they Germans – would they be loike to foight English women and their child'ern?*'

SOLDIER MAN: '*No-ah, Garge. Oi can't say they would.*'

FARMER'S MAN: '*Then I be goin' to foight they blokes as do. I be goon' to join th' Union.*'

FRANCIS CARRUTHERS GOULD

The Westminster Gazette   August, 1914

I find it hard to praise this cartoon too highly. It is laconic, elegant, powerful and it rams home its message without need of a caption or of anything but shadow. You can tell from the bulges of the side whiskers below the policeman's helmet (and from the familiar bulk) that Police Constable John Bull is about to catch Kaiser Bill the burglar. Belgium and Serbia as the family silver is a brilliant conception, and wartime allows cartoonists to be rude to foreign heads of state. The Germans called the Kaiser the 'All-Highest' but Gould gives him the features and the 'caught-in-the-act' pose of the common thief. Drama, morality and wit are all combined in this powerful and restrained cartoon.

At a stroke, the Germans become the thieving baddies and Britain is Europe's kindly, reliable bobby.

F. H. TOWNSEND

Punch   August 12, 1914

It would not be possible to attempt any collection of British cartoons without including this, one of the most famous of them all. Like Gould's burglar, the villainous old bully with his sausages and his big stick leads us to hate the Germans, and the plucky, clean-cut, defiant youngster brings out all our sympathy for the Belgian allies.

This cartoon idea has been used and borrowed and circulated endlessly. In July 1933, when Hitler was threatening to occupy Austria, *Punch* copied the Townsend idea, with a gallant little Austria before the same farm gate, and a bullying Hitler waving the same old stick. But they forgot the sausages.

BRAVO, BELGIUM!

BERNARD PARTRIDGE

Punch   August 26, 1914

The tone has hardened in the two weeks since 'Bravo Belgium'. The cartoonist is now using pure propaganda to convey the message that the enemy is wholly evil. Modern wars, which depend upon high civilian morale, need propaganda. *Punch* hurried to oblige. The rest of the British press was full of 'reliable' stories of the looting, raping, murdering Germans. Great play was made of the tale that German troops had removed the clappers from Belgian churchbells and hung nuns in their place. The yarn had about as much reliability as the equally popular story of the angel which had appeared to inspire some exhausted but valiant British soldiers at the great battle of Mons. The Angel of Mons was taken as clear proof that God was on our side. Similar nonsense filled the German press.

Remembering Partridge's taste for ambiguity, could that be an expression of regret on the German face?

THE TRIUMPH OF 'CULTURE'

WILL DYSON

The Herald   October 31, 1914

The war and the shortage of money had stopped daily publication of the *Herald*, and the name was accordingly changed. Dyson is again savaging one of his favourite targets, the Bloomsbury set liberal intellectuals. (D. H. Lawrence drew blood from the same type in *Women in Love* but he drew from the life of Lady Ottoline Morell.) Again it is the sharp, angular draughtsmanship which lifts this cartoon to the level of genius. Dyson could wring so much variety, suggest so many nuances of class, income and attitude from the hoary old trick of two people in conversation.

SACRIFICE

'Yes, darling, one feels that it is one's duty to set an example of self-denial to the people – I have put Fido and all the dear dogs on the same food as the servants.'

JACK WALKER

Daily Graphic   April 27, 1915

The crudity of bomb-aiming techniques in 1915 is alone sufficient for us to dismiss this cartoon as yet another expression of the way the cartoonists were volunteering, along with so many others, for the war effort. There is nothing surprising about this, all the nations were doing the same thing. It was only the men in the trenches who saw the irony of everybody claiming that right was on his side. They even made up a song about it which ended with a very confused God, deafened by prayers for both sides, saying 'Mein Gott, said God, I've got my work cut out'.

One of the remarkable things about this cartoon is the astonishing similarity between the schoolmaster-Civilization figure and that grand old man of British politics, W. E. Gladstone. He was dead by now, but his name and face lived on as the epitome of morality in public life. That, too, was a kind of propaganda, as we learned with the recent publication of his diaries, with little whip marks beside the accounts of his visits to prostitutes 'in order to save them'.

WILFULLY STUPID

CIVILIZATION: '*Your discriminating faculties seem at fault. Just commit those two examples to memory.*'

W. K. HASELDEN

Daily Mirror   May, 1915

This comes from a series by Haselden, called the 'Sad Adventures of Big and Little Willie' about Kaiser Bill and his weasel-faced son. (All the British cartoonists exaggerated the weasel quality but the Crown Prince was genuinely ferret-like in his heart and in his features. He claimed to have taken personal charge of the great slaughter at Verdun, so he deserved all the abuse he got.)

The Germans had hoped for great things from their Zeppelin airships and air bombardment. Soldiers always expect these things to do enormous damage, but as Britain and Germany found in the Second World War, prolonged bombing is not a war-winner and on occasion it can stiffen enemy morale. The Germans' air attacks were too few and their bombs too light to affect the war, although it did morale a great deal of good by convincing the civilians that they too were in the front line. Zeppelins were also quite easy to shoot down, once fighter planes had been developed that could catch them.

[Copyright—*The Daily Mirror*.

JANUARY – THE GREAT PLOT TO SCARE THE LION

The Willies felt they must do something to scare the horrid British Lion, for people were saying very uncomplimentary things, such as, that it wasn't a bit afraid of them. So they devised a sure remedy for this, and after six months brought all their Zeppelins to the front and even sent a Taube to drop a bomb on a cabbage garden at Dover. But the Lion only grinned at all their booing, and said: '*Send some more, but please spare the women and children.*'

E. T. READ

The Bystander   June 2, 1915

The *Bystander* was enormously popular with the troops. This was mainly because of another cartoonist called Bairnsfather, but the magazine was also noted for an acute political intelligence. This cartoon is prophetic. Once the Conservatives and the Liberals joined together in a war coalition, the fundamental changes in British politics which had been foreshadowed by Joe Chamberlain's departure from the Liberal Party and by the rise of the Labour movement, began to move steadily towards the two-party, Labour–Conservative giants of the future. And it was the war-time coalition which doomed the Liberals. Asquith (the shorter soldier with the long hair) was another casualty of the war; he never held office again, having been Prime Minister for ten years.

THE 'PALS'

AND THE GIRLS THEY LEFT BEHIND THEM

ONE OF THE GIRLS: '*Well, I suppose we've got to trust them to come back to us when it's all over, but, my dear! you know what men are, – it's a fearful risk!!!*'

This cartoon really came into its own during the Blitz on London in the Second World War, when *Punch* re-published it in 1941. But in 1915 it caught a popular mood, and Churchill's saying 'Business As Usual' became the kind of catch-phrase that explained away all the harassments of war. Perhaps Stampa did not make as much of the idea as he might. Apart from the forlorn chair on the heap of rubble, he could have draped other items of exploded stock around the splintered beams; an unharmed cauliflower perched in the ruins or even a surprised cat. Imagine what Giles would have done with this theme.

GRIT
The morning after the Zeppelin raid in our village

FRANK HART

Punch   January 26, 1916

The theme of war gives me an opportunity to bring into these pages
cartoonists like Frank Hart and Stampa who have little right to be
included in a collection of political cartoons. But the tradition of British
comic art is a happy and a forceful one and I wish there was room to
include some of the early work of Charles Keene, du Maurier and Phil
May. But Hart is a pleasant enough example, and this reference to
Germans as vermin is not only good propaganda but it also shows what
cartoon readers thought was funny in 1916. In the introduction to this
book I referred to a tradition of Populist cartoons, and argued that
Punch kept this kind of style away from its political pages. So it did, but
the style of the crowded, busy canvas, and the theme of the common
people was faithfully maintained by *Punch*'s comic artists. It was often
patronizing, with dialogue expressed in unlikely accents and grammar,
but it was usually good-hearted enough.

'*Us have had a letter from our Jarge. He've killed three Germans!*'
'*I bain't zurprised! Lor'! How that boy did love a bit o' rattin', or anything to do
with vermin!*'

The Conscientious Objector had a hard time in the First World War.
Almost invariably, he went to prison. But Quakers have always been
something of a special case; quite prepared to face the dangers of battle
as a stretcher-bearer or auxiliary, but determined not to fight. For *John
Bull* magazine, and its editor Horatio Bottomley, this was no excuse,
particularly when the Quaker-dominated cocoa trade boomed as a result
of the war. (For some reason, the troops loved it. In the Second World
War, it became an enormously popular hot drink with the Royal Navy.)

Bottomley became a professional jingoist, a man who made a habit of
touring the country making warlike speeches, weeping into the Union
Jack, and exerting every kind of moral blackmail to urge men to volun-
teer for the long slaughter of the Western Front. He ended up in prison
for fraud . . .

TAKING AND QUAKING

(*'Let not thy left hand know what thy right hand doeth.'* – Matthew vi, 3.)
The Quaker who is taking and the taker who is quaking.

BERNARD PARTRIDGE

Punch   August 2, 1916

The battle of the Somme had been raging for two months, and had cost more than 500,000 casualties (57,000 of them in the first two hours) when Partridge drew this. We have the national spirit of Erin with her funny speech, and Britannia has a modern armoured car to match her Roman helmet. He loved the old conventions, did Partridge – which is probably why, like Tenniel, he was awarded a knighthood.

The political root of this cartoon was in the Easter uprising of 1916 in Dublin, when the British Army put down a Republican rebellion. In 1914, although Home Rule for the Southern Irish counties had passed on to the statute book, there was a general agreement to drop the contentious subject for the duration of the war. But when overdue reforms are delayed, some of the reformists tend to become revolutionaries. By 1916, Home Rule was no longer enough for many Irishmen; they wanted Independence and a Republic. Partridge has noted a renewed agitation for Home Rule, and his cartoon suggests that war makes it untimely. The British government was more perceptive; it did not even try to introduce conscription in Ireland.

THE NON-STOP CAR

ERIN: '*Come on out o' that now, Darlint, or ye'll be kilt intirely.*'

L. RAVEN HILL

Punch   September 3, 1916

Raven Hill was Partridge's junior partner on *Punch*, and lived and drew in the old master's shadow. This cartoon looks like a Partridge, but Ravenhill later showed a boldness of line and a free imagination in design which makes him a major figure. Observe the noble British worker; purified by the crucible of war and no longer the dangerous Socialistic type of the Edwardian era (which was to re-emerge in *Punch* mythology in the 1920s).

The cringing German (you can tell by the Meerschaum pipe) worker is clearly hoping to get the American to weaken British morale. But as the *Punch* caption explains, the British worker is made of sterner stuff.

OUTSIDE THE PALE

AMERICAN LABOUR LEADER: '*Won't you meet your German comrade?*'
BRITISH TRADE UNIONIST: '*Yes, I'll meet him on the battlefield, but nowhere else.*'

FRANK REYNOLDS

Punch   September 27, 1916

Reynolds, another of the *Punch* comic artists, is making two points here:
British troop morale is magnificent, and he is well aware that the battle-
field of the Somme was a dreadful place to be fighting. There is also a
sly dig at the well-meaning nature of padres; although as Robert Graves
records in his autobiography, the only military chaplains who won the
troops' respect were the Catholics (and, less officially, the Salvation
Army) who stayed in the front-line with the men. The Anglican padres
tended to be backward in coming forward.

A fairly thorough check of First World War memoirs has found no
account of a concert being held at a casualty clearing station. They were
very near the front-line, and the wounded spent very little time there
before being returned to units, sent back to England, transferred to a
French hospital or buried. Perhaps Reynolds found one with a concert;
perhaps he felt the civilians needed a comforting view of the facilities
available for the wounded.

SCENE: Concert at a Casualty Clearing Station.
PADRE: '*Lance-Corporal Gascoyne, of the – Regiment, just in from the Somme, will sing "A Little Bit of Heaven".*'

LOUIS RAEMAEKERS

De Telegraf *(Holland)* *1916*

Raemaekers is not British, but he deserves inclusion because his cartoons were widely circulated in Britain as reassurance that a neutral agreed that God was indeed on our side. The British government also arranged for their wide circulation in the neutral USA, where they had a striking effect.

Raemaekers was a propagandist and a very good one. Like Dyson's visions of Germany, he portrayed the Germans as so totally evil that their opponents had to be wholly good. With hindsight, it is easy to see that Britain and Germany were similar kinds of societies; both were monarchies, they had overseas Empires, industrial economies, Labour movements, large exports. Doubtless the Germans would have retained any French soil they conquered, just as we snapped up their overseas Empire and retained it. German propaganda was equally outlandish.

THE ZEPPELIN RAIDER

BERNARD PARTRIDGE

Punch   August 15, 1917

Another classic Partridge cartoon; the man's eye for detail is magnificent, and the soldier's equipment is correct for the period down to the Mark 1 No. 4 Lee Enfield rifle. When going into battle the soldier would have more kit – on average, British soldiers attacked the German machine guns through barbed wire while carrying equipment with a total weight of 70 pounds.

That suspicious-looking character who is going to Stockholm was attending an International Socialist Conference at which representatives of the Labour movements of the warring powers tried to reach a peace settlement. Unknown to the general public, the warring governments were trying to do the same thing. But by this time, Britain and France were confident that the new American ally would enable them to win. The US more than made up for the loss of Russia, whose war effort was ended by the revolutions of February and October 1917. Newly Socialist Russia hoped that the Stockholm conference would lead to a general peace. This was clearly subversive, in *Punch*'s patriotic eyes.

THE REAL VOICE OF LABOUR

TOMMY: '*So you're going to Stockholm to talk to Fritz, are you? Well, I'm going back to France to* fight *him.*'

BRUCE BAIRNSFATHER

THE BYSTANDER 1917

(Two cartoons from the 'Fragments from France' collection)

This was perhaps the nearest thing to anti-war propaganda which the British media had to offer during the war. The cartoons were by a man who had fought in the trenches and who knew what that kind of wholly new warfare was like. Veterans of the Western Front have paid almost universal testimony to Bairnsfather as a historian of the conditions in which they fought and the sense of humour which the soldiers brought to bear against the life, or more precisely, against the death.

The two most famous Bairnsfather cartoons are too well-known to need inclusion; the archetypal soldier Old Bill muttering to his companion while they shelter in a shell crater: 'If you know a better 'ole, go to it'; and Old Bill sitting by a brick wall with a shell-hole in it and a new recruit asks what made that hole – 'Mice'.

These two cartoons speak for themselves. It should be noted that during the Paschendaele campaign of 1917, drowning in mud was a common cause of death.

F. H. TOWNSEND

Punch   September 5, 1917

This cartoon is a testimony, not to the success of the U-boat campaign, but to an odd obsession for hoarding goods which afflicted Britain late in 1917. The worst months of the war for the German submarine blockade was April, 1917, when one ship in four leaving British ports failed to return. The Germans were sinking 30,000 tons of shipping each day – ten times the rate at which new merchant ships could be built. Britain's reserve of wheat sank to a mere six weeks' supply. The answer was well-protected convoys of certain ships, and by the summer, the problem was clearly solved. But, ironically, the consumer began to panic, leading to the kind of shortages in the shops which this cartoon commemorates. A haphazard system of rationing quickly followed, which resulted in an appreciable rise in national food consumption, as people insisted on taking their full ration. With 'Tipperary' and 'Pack up your troubles in your old kitbag', the song Lloyd George is playing in the cartoon, 'Keep the home fires burning', became one of the major popular tunes of the war. It was rivalled by the songs from the most popular recent musical, 'Chu Chin Chow'.

'KEEP THE HOME FIRES BURNING'

SOLO BY OUR OPTIMISTIC PREMIER.

L. RAVEN HILL

Punch   November 28, 1917

Pacifist pamphlets were banned in this month, a blow to the freedom of the press in Britain which has left a lasting bruise. The same basic legislation was used to prosecute pacifists in the 1970s who informed soldiers of how they could become conscientious objectors.

Mr Punch's view of the pacifists speaks for itself. But there was little need for such rigorous methods of coercion. There was enough popular support for the war to ensure that three-quarters of the men who put on uniform were volunteers. When conscription began, the number of recruits fell, because a large number of key workers such as miners and engineers were prevented from volunteering.

BIRDS OF ILL OMEN

MR PUNCH: *'Only got him in the tail, Sir.'*
THE MAN FROM WHITEHALL: *'Yes, but I mean to get the next one in the neck.'*

L. RAVEN HILL

Punch   March 13, 1918

This cartoon speaks for itself. Industrial disputes on the Home Front were beginning to reach alarming proportions. The reason was, in part, fear of post-war redundancies.

The intriguing question about this and so many other Raven Hill cartoons is that they appeared to be aimed at that sector of the population – the industrial, organized working class – which almost certainly contained the tiniest proportion of *Punch* readers. But *Punch* cartoons were trend-setters, often plagiarized, adapted and sometimes re-printed in more popular publications.

The bulk of the Labour movement supported the war; Labour as a political force could be said to have come of age in December, 1916, when Arthur Henderson coolly informed Asquith that Labour would not follow him into the political wilderness. Labour would follow Lloyd George – the man who promised to get on with the war.

TOMMY (off to the Front – to ship-yard hand): '*Well, so long, Mate: We'll win the war all right if you'll see that we don't lose it!*'

FRANCIS CARRUTHERS GOULD

Westminster Gazette   November 28, 1918

In spite of the politicians' promises to build 'homes fit for heroes', some military units felt themselves so ignored and mistreated after the end of the war that a series of demobilization riots took place. There were mutinies in Rhyl, Calais and Folkestone. Horse Guards Parade was occupied by demonstrating troops. The Government surrendered and brought in the rule 'First in, First out'. With the end of the war, the Liberal Party itself finally split, between Lloyd George's supporters who continued the uneasy wartime coalition with the Conservatives, and the Asquith supporters who maintained their ideological purity, demanded a return to the old Liberal principles of Free Trade, and never formed a Government again. Lloyd George's contribution to the death of the Liberal Party made Labour the natural heir in the two–party system. Five years after the end of the war, Britain had a Labour Government, albeit a minority one, headed by a Prime Minister who had opposed the First World War.

THE SOLDIERS' VOTE

1st Tommy: *'What d'you think about this General Election? I see they've fixed it for December 14.'*

2nd Tommy: *'Well, I don't see why they're in such a hurry about it! It has taken us more than four years of hard fighting to put it through, and it seems to me they might have waited a few months longer to let us get home and see what we've got to vote for.'*

1st Tommy: *'At any rate, it didn't require a new Parliament to say "Thank You" to us.'*

DAVID LOW

The Star 1922

The industrial unrest of the early 1920s was matched by the renewed Irish crisis, as though the crises of 1912 and 1913 had waited courteously while the war raged, and then picked up again where they had left off.

But things had changed. There were tanks, there was a brilliant new cartoonist called David Low, and there was the unlikely Government coalition of Lloyd George and his Liberals and the increasingly disenchanted Conservatives. Low immediately began to picture the coalition as a two-headed ass. Still, it managed to 'solve' (or at least outflank) the Irish problem for a generation by offering the compromise of partition for Ulster and independence for the Southern Counties. It satisfied nobody, but as Low's tank suggests, nothing else seemed likely to work except an even nastier solution backed up by armed force.

THE PEACEMAKER

WILL DYSON

The Daily Herald   1919

Perhaps Dyson's most famous cartoon, and certainly one of the most prophetic. The 1940 class, the infants of 1919, were to fight another world war. Orlando of Italy, Clemenceau of France, Woodrow Wilson of the US and Lloyd George of Britain leave the Versailles conference hall. Perhaps their most important mistake was to insist that a defeated and humiliated Germany repaid the allies for the costs of the war. In so far as this could be achieved, it meant that Germany had to become a rich, prosperous nation to raise such vast sums. But an economically-prosperous nation was a strong nation, capable of mobilizing a military strength which would allow Germany to mock the reparations demands. Much of the history of the 1920s, and many of the causes of the Great Slump of 1929, could be traced to this elementary stupidity.

THE TIGER: '*Curious! I seem to hear a child weeping!*'

BERNARD PARTRIDGE

Punch   February 11, 1920

Although President Wilson was the father of the idea of the League of
Nations, a forum in which the nations' disputes could be peaceably
settled, the US Senate refused to allow America to join it. In the same
way, the US Treasury refused to help the economic recovery of war-
torn Europe, and drifted into a new isolationism. The other potential
super-power, backward and revolution-tossed Russia, also withdrew
from the European arena for most of the 1920s. Partly as a result,
Europe appeared once again to be the dominant centre of the world, as
it had been before 1914, but this time without the economic and military
dominance of the pre-war era. Left to its own inadequate resources,
Europe sought political solutions in Fascism in Italy, and bitter class
conflicts which paved the way for the extreme solutions of Nazism, civil
war in Spain, and in the unpleasant authoritarianism of Poland and the
Balkans.

ANOTHER 'RESERVATION'

STARVING EUROPE: *'God help me!'*

AMERICA: *'Very sad case, but I'm afraid she ain't trying.'*

F. H. TOWNSEND

Punch   April 7, 1920

The renewed outburst of trade union militancy after the war, with twenty-six million working days lost through strikes in 1920, and eighty-five million days lost in 1921 (compared with three million days lost in 1961) seemed to recall the dreadful industrial disputes of the years before the war. It took the defeat of the General Strike of 1926 to end the militancy. The eight million working days lost of 1929 was the worst year for strikes until the 1960s.

The nation, warned *Punch*, was facing bankruptcy through the greedy demands of the workers and their sinister political masters. The loutish bully of this cartoon is a far cry from the noble workman of *Punch* cartoons during the war. Times had changed.

'OLIVER "ASKS" FOR MORE'

MINER: *'You'll be sorry one of these days that you didn't give me nationalization.'*
PREMIER: *'If you keep on like this there won't be any nation left to nationalize you.'*

BERNARD PARTRIDGE

Punch   April 13, 1921

This is class war with a vengeance, with coats off and fists clenched. But it is important to remember that governments and employers were not deliberately wicked; economic orthodoxy said that wages had to be cut, men had to lose their jobs, and the unemployed had to wait until the divine laws of supply and demand got to work again. That was economic holy writ. John Maynard Keynes, a British economist, reckoned that prosperity could be brought back by Governments deciding boldly to spend money, create jobs and thus give people more money to buy more goods which would have to be produced by more factories employing more people. It was not until 1929 that politicians began to listen to him, and well into the 1930s, economic orthodoxy and mass unemployment prevailed, until the threat of war brought a re-armament boom.

UP AGAINST IT

CAPITAL TO LABOUR: '*You may succeed in knocking me out, but don't forget that then you'll have to fight a champion that no one can stand up against.*'

DAVID LOW

The Star 1922

Like so many of Low's cartoons, this speaks for itself. The two-headed coalition ass is there, with the war profiteers, the unemployed, the crushed taxpayer and Lloyd George, whom Low always endowed with a Puckish, mischievous air.

SPEAKING OF WAR MONUMENTS –

WILL HOPE

The Daily Herald   April 14, 1924

The coalition collapsed when the Conservative back-benchers, led by Stanley Baldwin, began to realize that their party did not need Lloyd George any more. A Conservative Government followed, which proceeded to lose a general election (by advocating unpopular tariffs) and Ramsay MacDonald's minority Labour Government took office.

The *Daily Herald* was no longer the dangerous revolutionary paper which had nurtured Will Dyson; it was now the authorized organ of the Labour movement, as we see in this perceptive cartoon about the difficulties facing MacDonald.

The political message is rather feeble. What is exciting is the clear association of the new technology of aviation and 'death rays' with some kind of progress. Will Hope, for one, sees that Britain is entering a new age, with new machines and new candidates for power. In the 1960s, Labour was again to identify itself with technological progress, with Harold Wilson's 'white hot heat of the technological revolution'.

Pilot Ramsay MacDonald finds himself up against a storm of 'Invisible Death Rays', of which we have been hearing lately, but they cannot stop his progress.

BERNARD PARTRIDGE

Punch   June 18, 1924

The British trade-union movement had a good two generations of his-
tory by the time of this cartoon; long enough for any institution to
develop hardening of the arteries and become vulnerable to new
militants. Unofficial strikes became a cause of concern in the 1920s,
until the unofficial strike leaders became the trade-union establishment
of the 1930s, and after the Second World War, yet a new generation of
unofficial strike leaders arose and began to win official power in their
turn. But the stunning aspect of this cartoon is Partridge's departure
from tradition with the inset picture of a comic-style John Bull, based
on the popular comic hero Felix the Cat. The new cartoons of Low and
Hope and the younger men were cracking the traditional *Punch* mould.

INFELIX keeps on walking.

LÈSE-MAJESTÉ

TRADE UNIONISM (to Unofficial Striker): '*This is not an ordinary strike – it's rank revolution. You're not merely defying your employers and the public – you're defying me!*'

(*Insert:* John Bull himself in training for a repetition of the recent strike.)

BERNARD PARTRIDGE

Punch   October 29, 1924

This was Partridge's contribution to the electorate's reasoned debate during the General Election campaign. A vote for Labour is a vote for the beastly, hairy Bolsheviks.

Partridge was not the only Conservative publicist to hit below the belt. Just before polling day, a letter was published, said to come from the pen of Zinoviev, President of the Communist International, ordering the British Communist Party to begin revolutionary and subversive work. It is now widely regarded as a crude forgery, and although Labour increased its popular vote, the Conservatives scooped up much of the benefit from the collapse of the Liberal vote and dominated the next parliament. The Red Letter and the anti-Bolshevik mania of the Conservative press set an unhappy tone for British political life.

The sign reads:

> VOTE
> FOR
> MACDONALD
> AND
> ME

ON THE LOAN TRAIL

STRUBE

Daily Express   May 19, 1926

The General Strike is over, the British Lion is victorious over the threat of massed trade-union action, and the cigar is back in the boss's smiling mouth. Note the police armband and truncheon on the desk, signs that our hero was a special constable during the Strike.

Strube's regular character, John Citizen, is back at work as a secretary, but sporting the inevitable walrus moustache.

BUSINESS AS USUAL
'Now where were we, Miss, when that fellow interrupted us?'

STRUBE

Daily Express   May 17, 1926

The air of triumph lingered in the Conservative press long after the General Strike collapsed. The Empire had won the battle against the enemy within, and was once more the wonder of the world. The victorious Conservative Prime Minister Stanley Baldwin becomes John Bull incarnate, contrasting vividly with Ramsay MacDonald's suspiciously foreign-looking striped shirt and moustaches. Winston Churchill takes the admission fees for the world's entry into that marvellous building, the Houses of Parliament fun fair. A happy John Citizen watches from the wings.

RAMSAY: '*Call yerself a showman; why, yer couldn't run a whelk stall.*'
STANLEY: '*Well, and who wants to run a whelk stall?*'

STRUBE

Daily Express   April 26, 1927

Women in the twenties, the Charleston-dancing flappers who smoked cigarettes in public, and wore their skirts and their hair short, were given the vote. Not that there were many flappers among the nation's young women, but it was a convenient label for a society which had only twenty years earlier fought hard against the idea of giving any woman the vote.

SHADE OF OLD MILITANT: '*So this is what I fought for!*'

STRUBE

Daily Express   October 12, 1927

It is almost as though the cartoonists revelled in the opportunity to draw
women who were not classic goddesses representing Peace or Germany
or the Spirit of Commerce. The Flapper passed into the stock-in-trade
of the political cartoonist, and it was a legitimate political question to
wonder whether they would vote almost *en bloc* for one party. There
were even fears that their vote would go to the most handsome, which is
doubtless the reason for Ramsay MacDonald preening his moustaches,
and Lloyd George's roguish glance. Nobody could ever accuse Stanley
Baldwin of being a ladykiller – which just went to show what a solid,
typical Englishman he was. The lettering on the horse reflects the
popular device in advertising and commercial art of the day to combine
words into purely visual images. Spratts 'Bonio' was one of the best-
known examples. This cartoon testifies at the same time to the sharpness
of Strube's daily eye and to the debt that commercial designers in all
fields were beginning to pay to the Expressionists and the *avant-garde* of
modern art.

THE DARK HORSE

DAVID LOW

Evening Standard   July 26, 1928

In 1927, David Low moved to the *Evening Standard*, attracted by a large salary and a solemn promise (and written contract) from Beaverbrook promising him freedom to draw as he pleased. This cartoon appeared on the day of the world championship fight between Gene Tunney and Tom Heeney, who was advised to use his footwork and keep well out of Tunney's reach.

Baldwin's response to a motion of censure in the Commons was to evade the question. The Government juggled with the definition of unemployment and imposed tougher restrictions on the granting of Unemployment Relief in an attempt to keep the statistics down. Churchill cheers Baldwin on from the corner, while Lloyd George and MacDonald make a bewildered appearance at the ringside.

THE BIG FIGHT

SPI

Reynold's Illustrated News   April 7, 1929

Winston Churchill, as Chancellor of the Exchequer, produced a useful pre-election budget which declared a modest surplus. This was very popular with the electorate until Philip Snowden did his sums and established that the surplus had come from some judicious juggling of the books, and the Sinking Fund had been the source of the surplus cash.

The cartoon is particularly apt because of Churchill's own passion for bricklaying. He boasted of the walls, cottages and swimming pools he had built. He even applied to become a member of the Bricklayers' Union but the TUC forbade it.

THE AMATEUR BRICKLAYER: *'There, that doesn't look so bad, and perhaps people won't notice that I've pinched the mortar.'*
(Mr Churchill has been bricklaying and Budget-making in the holidays. Mr Snowden, on another page, points out that his so-called surplus has been made by raiding the Sinking Fund.)

L. RAVEN HILL

Punch   September 24, 1930

This cartoon is timeless. It could have appeared in the 1970s, if Harold Wilson's face were substituted for that of MacDonald. The value of the dole at this time was just over sixteen shillings a week for a single man – hardly a princely sum. It was largely paid for by the workers themselves, through the insurance principle which Lloyd George introduced before the First World War. It was a condition of the international bankers, when the Labour Government needed a loan to shore up the pound during the financial crisis of 1931, that the money would only be made available if Unemployment Benefit were cut by ten per cent. This condition split the Labour Cabinet and Labour Party, and Ramsay MacDonald and his followers formed the National Government, a coalition with the Conservatives. The National Government solved the crisis by devaluing the pound – which the Labour Cabinet had thought to be impossible. The Treasury did not advise the Cabinet that it was one of the available options.

INDISCRIMINATE DOPE

THE HORSE (addressing John Bull): '*It's all right, Guv'nor. This isn't meant to make me try any harder. It's just a comforting drug.*'

JOHN BULL: '*If this goes on, somebody will have to be warned off the course.*'

DAVID LOW

Evening Standard   May 11, 1933

Crises came thick and fast in the 1930s. The collapse of the pound, of the Labour Government, and the great slump were quickly followed by the rise of Hitler and the growing threat of a new European war. Low was remarkably early to see the dangers of Hitler, dangers which he firmly believed to be inherent in any régime which based itself on racial hatred and on the suppression of free speech.

Rosenberg was the Nazi Party's token intellectual, the author of the Third Reich's bizarre racial theories about 'sub-human' Jews and Blacks.

THROUGH NAZI EYES

L. RAVEN HILL

Punch   March 4, 1931

Oswald Mosley was one of the most gifted young politicians of the 1920s. He was one of Labour's brightest hopes, in spite or because of his upper-class upbringing. He was unconvinced by the financial caution of the orthodox economists and worked endlessly to educate the Labour Party into the new age of Keynes's theories, which were to help pull America out of its 1930s depression. The Labour Movement was moved, and Mosley won many influential supporters, such as the miners' leader A. J. Cook. But the caution of the Labour leadership, and the orthodox views of MacDonald and J. H. Thomas, led them to suspect Mosley's recommendation as the kind of dangerous quack-cure that smacked of the mistrusted Lloyd George. Mosley resigned from the Cabinet in May 1930, two months after this cartoon. In 1931 he founded the New Party, which was an electoral disaster. In desperation, he then launched the British Union of Fascists, dressed his followers in black shirts and abandoned the mainstream of British politics. The kind of dramatic economic and political collapse which brought Hitler to power did not occur in Britain. Mosley had miscalculated.

OSWALD PUSHES OFF

Mr MacDonald: *'Why are you leaving the ship: it isn't sinking.'*
Sir Oswald Mosley: *'No: but it will be when I've done with it.'*

L. RAVEN HILL

Punch   January, 1933

People's minds were concentrated on the evils of mass unemployment, while Henry Ford's techniques of the assembly line and automated mass production made some 'experts' wonder if work would ever be found for everybody again. It was a common theme of the 1930s, even to the new medium of the cinema by Charlie Chaplin in *Modern Times*. But there is more than a hint of the old Puritan ethic that work is good for you – it was hard for people to realize that leisure could be a blessing when it was taken by choice, rather than by the brute force of mass unemployment.

THE SAVING OF LABOUR

THE ROBOT: '*Master, I can do the work of fifty men.*'
EMPLOYER: '*Yes, I know that, but* who is to support the fifty men?'

WYNDHAM ROBINSON

Morning Post   July 31, 1933

While Low warned about the dangers of dictatorship, there were many who joined Oswald Mosley in admiring their energy and drive and determination to get things done. Wyndham Robinson, one of the most talented cartoonists to emerge in the 1930s (his style shows what a dominance Low was beginning to exercise over the art) was far too intelligent to fall into that trap. He made the valid point that such Depression-beating energy could be mobilized quite as effectively by that other great democracy, the US, under Roosevelt and the New Deal. By comparison, MacDonald is an old woman. He was already beginning to go slightly senile; he would ramble embarrassingly at international conferences. Baldwin, as Robinson elegantly suggests, had other fish to fry.

'Come inside and shut the door, Stanley, that noise makes me feel quite faint.'

DAVID LOW

Evening Standard   September 12, 1933

The year of Hitler's accession to power, and Low sounds the same alarm as Will Dyson's anti-arms trade cartoon of 1913. It was the re-armament boom which later in the 1930s helped to pull the nation out of depression.

Potent though Low's message is, it is overwhelmed by the stunning force of this design. We can clearly see the influence of the twentieth-century painters in this cartoon, the symmetric beauty which the Futurists saw in machines, the bold and muscular lines of Leger. By comparison with this awesome power, Peace on her ice-cream cart has little chance.

COMPETING INDUSTRIES

DAVID LOW

Evening Standard   May 11, 1934

Mosley's Blackshirts were guaranteed to infuriate Low, and he summoned every great character from the British tradition of free speech and liberty to show why. Five months after this cartoon was published, a Fascist rally at Olympia, marked by the brutality of Mosley's stewards towards hecklers in the audience, began to swing public opinion in Low's direction. But in the summer of 1934, Low was almost alone in his opposition in the popular press; the *Daily Mail* gave Mosley regular and favourable publicity. One of the distinguishing marks of Low's style is his fondness for crowd scenes. Many fine cartoonists are happy with the simple conversation between two figures; Low loved the larger canvas, on which individual men seemed dwarfed by the greatness of the events of their time. He was inspired by the vast themes of mankind and its fate, rather than by the lone statesman or the straightforward political crisis. The 1930s, with its depression and dictators, gave him every opportunity.

PAGEANT OF LIBERTY AT RUNNYMEDE

POWELL

The Record   February, 1935

The Record was the journal of the Transport and General Workers Union, run by that Godfather of the British Labour Movement, Ernie Bevin. He was the dominant figure of the new style of British trade unionism in the years after the General Strike. It called for freedom from Government intervention, freedom for the unions to use their collective bargaining power to wring the best possible deal of pay and conditions from management. It was a pragmatic, non–doctrinaire trade unionism, and its success was an important factor in the survival and resurgence of the British Labour Party after the split of MacDonald's cabinet in 1931.

As the creator of the union coalition which became the TGW, Bevin was a man ahead of his time in the tactics of maintaining unity – the idea of a union journal was his and he was one of the few men in public life to be a convinced Keynesian in economics. Powell's cartoon may be stylistically tame and old-fashioned, but the very fact of its appearance in a union journal is a breakthrough.

LLOYD GEORGE: '*Let me give you a "New Deal" with these?*'
CHORUS FROM CARRIAGE: '*No thanks. We're having a "Square Deal" with these cards and on* THIS TABLE.'

WYNDHAM ROBINSON

Morning Post   April 8, 1935

Here the Foreign Secretary, Sir John Simon, and the young Anthony
Eden shower Europe with pacts, alliances, agreements, protocols and
treaties.

One of the commitments of the Treaty of Versailles which ended the
First World War was that henceforth, international relations should be
governed by 'open agreements, openly arrived at'. France promptly
allied herself with almost everybody; while Britain fought shy of alli-
ances, but happily signed pacts and agreements which guaranteed almost
every frontier in Europe. It amounted to much the same thing, but did
not sound so dangerous. When the crunch came, these treaties and pacts
proved to be less than binding. Czechoslovakia's alliances were worth
little when Hitler invaded, just as the great powers' promises not to
intervene in the Spanish Civil War were quickly broken. Britain and
France went to war in 1939, not for the sake of alliances, but because it
was clear that only a war would stop Hitler from dominating the whole
continent of Europe.

A GLIMPSE OF THE FUTURE
Mass Production of Pacts Subdues Europe

STRUBE

Daily Express   July 24, 1935

David Low may have seen the *Daily Express* as the regular paper of
Colonel Blimp, but Strube the cartoonist had no illusions about the
methods of the Nazi government, and this cartoon is a sharp rebuke to
the British Legion delegation which toured Germany on what became
almost a state visit.

The Steel Helmets (Stahlhelm) were a paramilitary group whose role
in German politics was quickly taken over by the Nazi Party's own
stormtroopers.

Interestingly, the only one of the Nazis' victims who appears to be
fighting back in this cartoon is the Jew.

PHOTOGRAPHER: *'The last photograph, sir. Kindly look this way, please.'*
         (*The British Legion delegation arrive home today.*)

STRUBE

Daily Express   September 5, 1935

Ernie Bevin, suitably portrayed as the Big Oyster, curtly dismisses Communists and their influence from the TUC annual conference at Margate. Bevin was anti-Communist, although not quite as firmly as Strube suggests here, because he knew full well that the Marxist tradition in the British Labour Movement was tiny and almost wholly irrelevant. But the real event of this TUC conference was the ringing decision to oppose Italy's invasion of Abyssinia, even at the risk of war. And Bevin, whose influence within the Labour Party was now massive, bulldozed aside the old pacifist and party leader, George Lansbury. Attlee replaced him and the policy of collective security knew its finest hour, as sanctions were imposed upon Italy. Mussolini was able to ignore them, because the vital commodity – oil – was not put on the sanctions list.

Tenniel, Strube and Garland in today's *New Statesman* have all borrowed scenes from 'The Walrus and the Carpenter'; it is a useful myth to use.

BY THE T.U. SEA

The largest oyster glared at him,
Plain were the words he said:
The largest oyster winked his eye,

And shook his heavy head –
Telling 'em clear as clear could be
To leave the oyster bed.

(After Lewis Carroll)

Daily Mail   March 10, 1936

Baldwin's Government, having fought the 1935 election on the popular platform of collective security and no great re-armament, soon changed its policy. Indeed, Baldwin was to confess that he had planned to re-arm while professing he would do no such thing. The woolly-minded Lib-Lab twins made what political capital they could from it, but with Bevin already convinced of the need to oppose the dictators, and the Spanish Civil War looming on the horizon, the Labour Movement ponderously and reluctantly began to accept that even collective security might need re-armament and even war.

Poy was a prolific cartoonist – he published some 10,000 in the course of his long career with the *Manchester Evening Chronicle*, the *Evening News* and the *Daily Mail*. He loved to create 'characters', like Government Gus (sitting on John Bull's cart) and the archetypal civil servants Dilly and Dally. He had been one of the great Redbaiters of the 1920s.

THE WOOLLY-MINDED TWINS: '*It's a positive outrage leaving the dear old homestead – AND FOR NO REASON WHATEVER!*'

WYNDHAM ROBINSON

Morning Post   June 9, 1936

The failure of economic sanctions to stop Mussolini's invasion of
Abyssinia was a key event in the growing disillusionment with tactics of
non-violence as a means of stopping dictators prone to violence. Oil
sanctions, which might well have stopped Italy's war effort, were never
tried. The month before this cartoon was published, the Emperor Haile
Selassie had fled Abyssinia; the Italians had won. The day after the
cartoon appeared, Neville Chamberlain called sanctions 'the very mid-
summer of madness'. No major statesman was prepared to defend the
use of sanctions again, until Harold Wilson vainly applied them against
Rhodesia in 1965.

L'ENFANT TERRIBLE

STRUBE

Daily Express   November 4, 1936

War in Spain, German troops back in the Rhineland, a Popular Front government in France – Strube was right to show the Jarrow marchers overshadowed by the threat of war. And although there were still one and a half million unemployed in 1936, they tended to be concentrated in the traditional areas of heavy industry. The new engineering industries of the Midlands and the expanding London suburbs were prospering and hiring more staff. Unemployment by 1936 was no longer the cause of a great slump hitting the whole economy, but of the long, lingering decline of the manpower-intensive industries which had been the original basis of the industrial economy – mining, shipbuilding, iron and steel. The towns of Northern England and Wales and Scotland which had grown up around these industries continued to suffer until the war boom of 1940. But they were far from the capital of London, and although the hunger marchers always found sympathy, there was rarely work.

THE TRAVEL THE ROAD
(Jarrow unemployed march to London to petition the Government.)

The Communist Party in Britain was too small to justify this cartoon. But the success of Communism and Popular Fronts in Europe was perhaps more frightening to the readers of the Conservative *Morning Post* than the Fascist and Nazi dictatorships against which the Popular Fronts were mobilized. The Civil War in Spain, between Franco and the Republic, seemed to be a microcosm of the impending ideological battle in Europe. Soviet Russia, and to a lesser extent the French Popular Front Government, supported the Republic, while Hitler and Mussolini poured modern aircraft, tanks and volunteers into the Spanish battlefield.

Within this context, the hunger-marchers appeared threatening in Britain, but their impact was psychological more than political. They were one more factor, like the almost Marxist writers – Spender, Auden, Day-Lewis – in the girding-up for war.

THE END OF THE TRAIL

GILMOUR

The Blackshirt 1936

The simplistic British Fascist solution to the problem of unemployment was to deport the foreigners. It is a sign of the ideological poverty of the movement that it should advocate sweeping remedies such as this when the Fascist leader Mosley had been one of the few British politicians correctly to analyse the economic problems and to point to the sophisticated measures which could overcome them.

It is a raw and amateur cartoon, the use of the New Broom metaphor lacks freshness. The dapper, neat appearance of the unemployed man suggests the lack of an eye for detail. Although Fascism was to retain a foothold in the East End of London even after the Second World War, its hopes of achieving political significance on a national scale had ebbed by late 1934, when Lord Rothermere and other influential backers began to disassociate themselves. There were street fights and parades to come, but not a hint of power.

BRITAIN FOR THE BRITISH

On the other hand, the low type of foreign Jew together with other aliens who are debasing the life of this nation, will be run out of the country in double-quick time under Fascism – *Extract from 'The Blackshirt'*.

The Abdication was the one issue over which the Fascist party and the British Communist party were able to demonstrate side by side, on behalf of a popular King. By the time they and the British public got to know of the King's love for a divorced woman, Baldwin had virtually settled the matter. The foreign press had been writing of the affair for months, but the story did not break in Britain until Decemer 2, after the Bishop of Bradford let it be known that the King was in need of God's Grace. The Abdication took place on December 11, and although there were some romantic moves to form a King's party to keep him on the throne, the Church, the Labour Opposition and the entire Cabinet (which threatened to resign if their advice were not followed) constituted an argument which the King could not ignore.

THE CHOICE

THE PRIME MINISTER: '*All the peoples of your Empire Sir, sympathize with you most deeply; but they all know — as you yourself must — that the throne is greater than the man.*'

ILLINGWORTH

Punch   September 21, 1938

It is almost ungallant to *Punch* and to Chamberlain to reproduce this tribute to Appeasement. Europe had been on the brink of war; gas masks had been issued in London, and trenches dug in Hyde Park. And then came the Munich settlement and the collective sigh of relief. It is hindsight, and perhaps the prescience of prophets such as Low, which lead us to mock the Appeasers today. But the feeling that almost anything was better than war (particularly a war as long and as costly as 1914–18) and that Germany did have legitimate complaints against the Peace of Versailles, was a testimony to fairness in British public life. It is, however, worth recalling that Chamberlain had taken out insurance in February, 1937, when he announced a £1,500 million re-armament programme. By the outbreak of war, Britain was producing each month as many tanks and more war planes, than Hitler's Germany.

STILL HOPE

WILL DYSON

Daily Herald   January, 1939

In the month of his death, Dyson produced this, one of the few great works (deserving comparison with his early cartoons) which he drew after he was devastated by the death of his young wife in 1919.   He has caught the authentic tone of Mae West's drawling, suggestive lines. Peace is sweetly innocent by comparison . . . nice girls come last. Dyson takes one of the classical cartoon symbols, the gentle maiden Peace, then transforms and exalts her by putting her in the wholly different context of Mae West, the whore of war. And there is a profound truth in showing how dangerous, but challenging and lusty war can be, compared to the virtuous charms of peace.

"THE NATIONS, THEY ALL LOVE ME —
AND PAY HOMAGE TO MY NAME"

"WELL SISTER — THEY MAYN'T LOVE ME —
BUT I GET THERE JUST THE SAME!"

SCOTT JOHNSTON

The Militant   June, 1939

The influence of the American cartoonists of the 1930s upon their British counterparts tended to be filtered through the observant eye of David Low, who followed the work of other cartoonists around the world. But occasionally they were re-printed in Britain, and Johnston's brilliant scene of confrontation shows how alert cartoonists abroad could be to the developing trends of modern art.

The Militant was the journal of the tiny and almost insignificant sect, the Militant Labour League. It must have been a confusing experience, being a committed left-wing revolutionary in 1939; obviously Hitler was a bitter ideological foe who had to be opposed; but war was clearly a capitalist plot against the workers, and after August, 1939, when Hitler and Stalin signed their non-aggression pact, loyal Communists had to stand on their heads to explain why Hitler was a deadly enemy last week, and an acceptable neighbour today.

WYNDHAM ROBINSON

Morning Post   March 9, 1937

This is doubtless a very unfair cartoon, but it is cunningly effective. It was a theme which was to find its political echo in 1945, in a bizarre electoral broadcast in which Winston Churchill attempted to warn the electorate that a Labour Government under Attlee would bring in the kind of authoritarian controls which Britain had just fought a war to defeat. Churchill even suggested that the London School of Economics professor, Harold Laski, would be a kind of British Himmler. The broadcast probably did Churchill more harm than good – Attlee and Labour had fought too hard against Hitler for that kind of mud to stick. Significantly, Robinson's 1933 approval of the energy and drive of the two dictators has now been replaced by revulsion.

FOLLOW MY LEADERS

ANON

Evening Standard (forgery) *1940*

This cartoon and the next come from a German propaganda version of the *Evening Standard*, air-dropped into Britain to spread false information and to undermine morale. The news columns are filled with the 'inside story' of Chamberlain's illicit share dealing, with the number of Jewish relatives by marriage of various Cabinet members, with subtly-phrased 'news' of British soldiers' wives being evicted by grasping landlords while the soldiers languish with inadequate equipment in France. The major thrust of the propaganda is class-based; the war was fomented by the upper class and by Jewish financiers, and ordinary English folk should steer clear of it.

By comparison with the care taken in choosing the news stories, the first cartoon appears crude and doomed to fail as propaganda. It is a barely recognizable caricature of Chamberlain.

It is not known how many copies were dropped by the Germans; only one is known to have survived.

CHAMBERLAIN: *'No admittance! All seats reserved for the ruling class and their friends.'*

ANON

Evening Standard (forgery) *1940*

The attack on the Jewish Minister Hore-Belisha is very much more effective, although I am far from sure how many *Evening Standard* readers would be familiar with the Latin tag of the old Roman gladiators 'We who are about to die salute thee, Belisha.'

To the British public, Belisha was best known for giving his name to the orange lights which marked zebra crossings. He had been sacked from the post of Secretary for War by Chamberlain in January 1940 because he correctly claimed that the British Army's defence lines were inadequate. Chamberlain was going to make him Minister of Information but Lord Halifax claimed this would be improper since Belisha was a Jew. He was an able man, who was doomed to remain out of office throughout the war. Ignorant of the ins and outs of British politics the Nazi cartoonist may have been, but he knows enough to equip Churchill with a cigar and Chamberlain with his umbrella.

AVE BELISHA, MORITURI TE SALUTANTI

E. H. SHEPARD

Punch   September 25, 1940

Shepard is perhaps best known as the illustrator of *The Wind in the Willows*, and the comparison between the loving detail with which he drew Mole and Toad and the furious bold strokes of the Rock and the Storm is remarkable in itself. There are a number of famous cartoons to commemorate 1940 and the close-run-thing of the Battle of Britain. There is Low's defiant British Tommy, shaking his fist at the whole of Europe and muttering 'Very well, alone'. There are any number of heroic Churchills, and anxious glances out to sea or up into the air. The strength of Shepard's work is the way he presents the conflict as a battle of elemental forces; the energy of the storm, the endurance of the rock. And the very terms he uses bear their own coded message – storms pass, but rocks remain. He has deliberately avoided the bulldogs and lions of the *Punch* tradition; for Shepard, the moment is too serious and the difference between the foes too profound, for those familiar devices.

THE ROCK AND THE STORM

STRUBE

Daily Express   *November, 1940*

The bombs have dropped, the windows have been shattered and Strube's familiar John Citizen, with gas mask and tin helmet, is subjected to the madness of war. But all is not lost. The wife knits busily in the shelter; she and her husband talk at cross purposes; the prize marrow is safe; the rainwater still runs into the barrel – the important things do not change.

This is a brilliant cartoon, funny and comforting and assertively British. It builds morale and it mocks the bombs of the enemy.

'Is it all right now Henry?'
'Yes, not even scratched'

ZEC

Daily Mirror   March 6, 1942

The 'price of petrol' cartoon almost got the *Daily Mirror* banned. It was interpreted by the Government as a threat to morale, a foul innuendo that the petrol companies were making vast profits out of dying sailors.

Zec himself later explained that it was part of a series about the black market and the dangers of wasting food or petrol. The explanation was accepted by the authorities, but the *Mirror* was given an official warning and the offending cartoon was debated in Parliament.

'The price of petrol has been increased by one penny' – OFFICIAL

GABRIEL

February 11, 1943

Hitler's invasion of Russia in 1941 was a military blunder; it was also a shot in the arm for the British war effort. Communist trade unionists put their considerable skills and effort into increasing production, and the fact that Russia suffered by far the heaviest casualties and mobilized the greatest armies of the Allies made the Russian alliance genuinely popular in Britain. It was the urge to help the Russians that gave the 'Second Front Now' campaign its force from 1942.

Note the strength of Low's Colonel Blimp, turning up in another cartoonist's work, with his 'Gad, Sir' and long moustaches. Gabriel, a distinguished cartoonist for the *Daily Worker*, had to publish elsewhere when the Government (in the person of the Labour Home Secretary Herbert Morrison) banned the paper in 1941. The Communist Party had organized a demonstration against the war, under the guise of a demand for more air-raid shelters.

WHOSE THE GAIN?

MOON

Sunday Dispatch 1943

Moon, a veteran of the *Daily Worker*, made no bones about his hatred of the Germans. But his was a common attitude among British cartoonists. Hitler had come to power quite legally in Germany; all of the evidence of the 1930s suggested that although he imprisoned, silenced or murdered his more vocal opponents, the majority of the German people were his loyal supporters.

GOOD AND BAD GERMANS

GABRIEL

July 2, 1943

After the experiences of the Blitz and the raid on Coventry, the British public was understandably delighted when the RAF and the US Air Force began its round-the-clock strategic bombing campaign on Germany. It was cheerfully recalled that Goering had once said if a single bomb fell on Berlin, you could call him Müller. The truth emerged long after the war that the amount of money, effort, manpower and raw materials put into the British bombing campaign probably took more out of the British war effort than it damaged the Germans. Certainly at the time this cartoon was published, the American daylight raids were suffering almost unacceptable casualties, in spite of their heavily-gunned Flying Fortresses, and the RAF night bombing campaign had still not achieved the kind of accuracy which made the heavy losses 'worthwhile'.

THE FUEHRER'S SORROW

145

LOW

Evening Standard   September 7, 1943

One of the first British cartoons to attack racism, and once again, Low leads the way. Racism spread its own poison among the American troops stationed in Britain, who were almost invariably segregated. There were a handful of instances, quickly covered by censorship, in which white and black GIs attacked each other with guns and grenades. Britain suffered from an incomprehensible ambiguity about race. When they fought beside us, there was no praise too high for the Ghurkas, Maoris and Indian Divisions. The troops mixed happily enough in the Western desert and when fighting the Japanese. The tolerance stopped however in civilian life. I find this hard to understand.

IMPERIAL WELCOME

GILES

Sunday Express   April 23, 1944

This is not a political cartoon. It is included because it expresses almost perfectly the muddled way Britain reacted to the three million American servicemen who passed through the country. They were rash, confident, good-humoured, friendly, generous with cigarettes, wealthy enough to afford taxis and somehow very different. The conventional phrase for the Americans, that they were 'overpaid, over-sexed and over here' is slickly misleading.

The reason the cartoon is only *almost* perfect is that the Berlin street scene lacks a curvaceous Fraulein and the wolf whistles that she would have provoked.

'TAXI!'

LOW

Evening Standard   August 9, 1945

The speed with which Low invariably seized on the salient point of any great political event is quite extraordinary. While most people were still trying to understand what an atom bomb did, apart from blow things higher than they had ever been blown before, Low perceived the ambiguity of the power, the choice of life or death, of destruction or of the harnessing of its incredible power for the purposes of peace. Although cartoonists have often used a baby to represent humanity. Low seems also to use the baby to suggest that mankind might be too immature to handle the choice science had presented.

'BABY PLAY WITH NICE BALL?'

STRUBE

Daily Express   November 26, 1945

Peacetime is back again. John Citizen is no longer the quiet civilian hero who can stand anything the enemy throws at him. He has reverted to type; put-upon, battered, always the victim. Nor were the strikes widespread enough to justify Strube's anger – 1946 and 1947 were reasonably quiet years for industrial relations with 2·1 and 2·4 million working days lost – about half the figure for 1944.

THE MAN WHO ALWAYS PAYS

E. H. SHEPARD

Punch   May 15, 1946

Cartoons themselves can become myth, and the famous Tenniel drawing of Bismarck being dismissed by the young Kaiser in 1890 captioned 'Dropping the Pilot' was well-enough known and a perfect enough image for the planned withdrawal from Egypt to fit happily into the convention. It was ten years before Egypt really controlled the keys to the Suez Canal, but Shepard has caught an important truth, that one of the major casualties of the war was the Empire itself. India was granted independence the next year, and within twenty years of the war's end, the largest Empire the world had known had been freely given back to the people who were colonized. It was not always a tidy job, and too many lives were wasted in the process, but compared with any other dismemberment of an Empire, the job was done with astonishing speed and with more than a passing regard for the stability and prosperity of the new nations that were left behind.

CLEOPATRA AND THE LION

ILLINGWORTH

Punch   June 12, 1946

London's victory parade down the Mall, and the two vital elements in the Allied victory were not present. Illingworth, perhaps borrowing a leaf from Partridge's book, is ambiguous about his own feelings. Is this a simple tribute to an ally, or a suggestion that the Bomb and the Bear are equally dangerous and deserve careful observation in the future?

AMONG THOSE ABSENT

OSBERT LANCASTER

Daily Express   July 25, 1948   November 12, 1948

The Americans in post-war Britain were civilians once more, whereas austerity Britain was still stuck in some twilight state between peace and war. With luxury goods (when they were made) reserved for the export market, and shortages of fuel and rationing of food, Britain in the late 1940s was a gloomy place and the glow of victory did not last long. British troops continued to die in Palestine and later in Korea. Taxes seemed to remain as high as ever. In fact, reconstruction was taking place at an astonishing rate and the transition to a peace-time economy was skilfully handled – and combined with full employment. But Britain was a country still scarred by war, as Lancaster's guide makes plain.

The style of the pocket cartoon, which Lancaster has elevated to folk art, is one of the most difficult to achieve. The space is so tiny and narrow, that the convention of two people conversing is almost forced. But nobody ever squeezed more from it than Lancaster, who managed to create and describe an entire family and keep them topical for thirty years.

"Darling, how does one entertain Americans? . . . If one gives them Spam and doesn't change, we're a down-at-heel, C3 nation, dying of malnutrition, while if one blows the week's meat ration and wears a new frock one's shamelessly abusing Marshall aid!"   12.xi.48

"Turn left where it says 'No cigarettes', keep straight on past wot used to be the petrol pump till you sees a notice saying 'No admittance by order of the War Office', and that's the old Elizabethan Manor 'ouse."   25.viii.48

VICKY

drawn for the *News Chronical* but unpublished

Vicky came to dominate the post-war period of cartoons as only David Low had done before him. He and Low had much in common; a basic humanitarianism which ran through all their work, a healthy mistrust of all those who sought power, and an instinctive loathing of bullies.

Truman's invitation to Attlee, that he might be led up the clearly signposted garden path into the flower bed where dollars are marked as the seeds of war, suggests that Vicky sees the American offer of friendship as suspect in itself. Stalin's rose garden, on the other hand, looks positively innocent.

COME INTO THE GARDEN, CLEM

The Labour Party had always included a Marxist wing; it was an inevitable part of being a coalition of the Left. But the man who was picked out as its leader had a heavy cross to bear. The Party's purists saw him as responsible for its ideological soul; its pragmatists saw him as responsible for its unity. Nye Bevan, expelled from the Labour Party before the war for his faith in the Popular Front, became one of its key figures thereafter. He was on the Left, but his leadership of that wing was due more to their personal fondness of him and his eloquence than to any ideological mastery.

As the Cold War became arctic, Marxism became a dangerous label for a British politician. It alarmed the American allies as much as it attracted the Left. Ironically, the ascetic Stafford Cripps, once Labour's great Left ideologue, is portrayed as part of the horrified 'moderate' circle around Bevan.

THE MAN WHO MENTIONED KARL MARX AT A SOCIALIST
GET-TOGETHER ... AND LIKEWISE –

ILLINGWORTH

Punch   April 5, 1950

Again there is the constant image of austerity. Illingworth shows clear confidence in at least one aspect of the Welfare State, but points to the bitter choices which national poverty imposes. The young Barbara Castle made the same point in the popular press – that Britain could afford to be a great scientific power or a great military power, but not both. The answer was that in the age of the Bomb, a great scientific power would automatically wield great military authority. Whether decent housing meant less need for hospitals is another matter.

PREVENTION IS BETTER...

(Estimated additional expenditure on National Health Services for 1950 –
£129 millions.
Proposed reduction in expenditure on Housing for 1950 – £24 millions.)

DAVID LOW

Daily Herald   January 12, 1951

America was an uncomfortable ally when its more bellicose politicians began to react to what they saw as the West's major defeat (when China was taken by Mao and the Communists, and Korea began to assume the status of some Holy War).

Men like Low, and many in the Labour Party, were deeply uncertain of the wisdom of taking America's part in the Cold War. But as Low pointed out, if a choice had to be made, then at least the US conducted its witch hunts in public.

LOW

Daily Herald   February 13, 1951

Low began to concentrate on the hard political decisions that had to be taken during the Cold War. Should Britain spend its limited resources on re-arming? Should it join the American crusade against Communism, and was it reasonable to justify the American alliance with the comforting thought that perhaps Britain could blur the increasingly sharp lines that divided Communism and the West? They were questions which wracked the Labour Movement, and although Low faced bravely up to his duty to give some kind of answer, the quality of his cartoons began to suffer.

GABRIEL

Daily Worker   April 27, 1953

Churchill lingered and lingered in office, while his health failed to the point where he was dropping off to sleep in the Cabinet. The junior Tory leaders who hoped to succeed him despaired of ever getting the old man to go. Eden was the heir apparent, but R. A. Butler and Harold Macmillan were promoting their own claims.

None of them, interestingly, seems to fit into the Churchillian clothes they are all trying on for size except Macmillan.

Now, Sir Winston, remember the motto of the Knights of the Garter — evil to those who evil think!'

GILES

Daily Express   July 9, 1955

The delight of a Giles cartoon lies in the loving care with which he
fleshes out a cartoon, packing it with details which make the scene ring
true. In the mob of cyclists coming from the gate, one has lost his
balance, and a smash is building up behind. The cyclist in the foreground
has a sun-tanned face – it is July and he is back from his early
holiday. The robot's electric plug trails behind. Giles loves to fill his
cartoons with people; whatever theme he chooses he tells it through the
eyes of human beings with whom we can sympathize. This is a cartoon
about automation, but Giles takes us out of the laboratory, out of the
work environment, and shows us a new, more personal threat. And he
wraps the threat in absurdity until it seems no threat at all. But the
overtime is still lost; the jobs are still threatened. We grin but we worry.

'Doing me out of overtime's one thing – riding home with Popsy's another.'

CUMMINGS

Daily Express   January 7, 1957

The skill of Cummings lay in his mastery of caricature – he could draw
every politician with malicious precision, could wring any expression he
chose from any face – and he combined this skill with combative political
views. Cummings was an aggressive, not an analytical, cartoonist. His
cartoons were rarely funny – they were political bludgeons. The UN
was unlikely to agree with British policy over Suez; the UN was there-
fore a haunt of knaves and horse traders. Anthony Eden had stood up for
British interests, which by definition had to be right; so his opponents
were feeble-minded subversives. It was a simple, moral universe to
inhabit, and a merciless one.

'*Justice?!! You won't find justice on ANY floor here.*'

VICKY

Evening Standard   December 11, 1958

Vicky's mocking attack on Macmillan as Supermac rebounded when the
Prime Minister welcomed the title, and the loyal Tory cartoonists took
up the chorus. And any politician who could hold the Conservative
Party together after the civil war on the back benches, which followed
the Suez débâcle, had some claim to the title. So Vicky changed his
attack, and struck home with the image of Archie Rice, '*The Entertainer*',
the sad clown hero of a John Osborne play which was then popular.
The guise of the faded Edwardian showman, game at heart, a profes-
sional to his fingertips, but never well-endowed with talent – this was a
label which stuck to Macmillan, emphasizing the pathos of those sad,
sloping eyes.

THE ENTERTAINER

TIMOTHY BIRDSALL

Private Eye June, 1963

The court of Emperor Harold Macmillan, as exposed by Christine Keeler, the Profumo scandal, the Vassall scandal, the shamed realization that Britain had not been consulted when Kennedy risked nuclear war over the Cuban missile crisis. Lust for young women, homosexual lust, lust for money, for honours, seemed to pollute the last months of Macmillan's government. Scandal followed upon scandal with a speed that made the nation punch-drunk. Birdsall's gift was to draw the whole astonishing spectacle without disgust and without prurience. It was there, some of it was to be enjoyed, and much of it was to be goggled at, but its exposure in ostensibly staid, self-controlled Britain was a delight and a miracle in itself. The old order was visibly rotting, and enjoying itself too.

the last days of
MACMILIAN

ZEC

Daily Mirror   October, 1959

Perhaps the most famous electoral slogan was one which Harold Macmillan, the Conservative Prime Minister, never quite said – 'You've never had it so good'. It sparked dozens of retorts of which Zec's was the most pointed at the time. It later became a national catch-phrase to describe what was called the affluent society. Although the bulk of the population was more prosperous and more likely to be in work than ever before, it suggested a careless complacency about those groups, like the pensioners or the disabled or the growing number of immigrants, who were falling through the wide gaps in the net of the consumer society.

167

TROG

Private Eye   July, 1963

Macmillan never really lived down the cheery slogan of the 1959 election 'You've never had it so good'. The Profumo scandal, with its accompanying rumours of depravity in high places, political orgies and sexy romps around the Cliveden swimming pool, portrayed the Conservative Party in a wholly new light. Had it not been for the fact that Profumo lied to the Commons about his affair with Christine Keeler, and had there not been a security risk in the generous girl's willingness to sleep with the Russian naval attaché while also bestowing her favours on the British Minister for War, he might have got away with just a roguish reputation. As it was, I'm not sure how much political harm it all did, when *Private Eye* ran happy cartoons of Miss Keeler coyly observing 'Life's better under a Conservative'. Labour seemed a boring lot by comparison.

VICKY

Evening Standard   October 19, 1964

Three days as Prime Minister, and already Wilson's pipe is sufficient identity for a cartoon character. But this is one of Vicky's less precise sketches of Wilson. The hair is wrong, the bags under the eyes are too marked (and Vicky later dropped them) and the mouth is not Wilson. Vicky, like Abu of the *Observer* later, was able eventually to draw a perfect Wilson, based upon short stature, a jauntiness of step and manner, a Boy Scout-ish air of straightforwardness that covered the slyness beneath. The economic crisis of 1964 (caused by a deficit of £800 million left by the defeated Conservative Government's naked attempt at winning votes with a pre-election boom) was less Wilson's baby than his permanent alibi. But Vicky's talent for prophecy was at work again – the over-riding issue of the Wilson years was Britain's dismal economic performance – and as the 1960s wore on, there was little doubt that if Wilson had not been the natural father of economic crisis, then he had certainly taken out adoption papers and given the abandoned child his name.

RALPH STEADMAN

Punch 1963

The fall-out from the Profumo scandal is all crammed together in the one house. On the ground floor is the brothel with the birds and the bottles and – of note – the hospital-style beds. Above them are the spies and in the next room are the immigrants crowded together into slum rooms. On top of the heap is the property developer, the slum landlords who made fortunes from terrorizing the sitting tenants until they fled their homes, when the immigrants would be packed in, until the profitable site was ripe for re-development.

It was through the girls in the Profumo scandal, and their friendship with one of the most notorious of these slum landlords, Peter Rachman, that the whole sordid story of the developers and their bullying tactics began to emerge.

'. . . that lived in the house that Jack spilt.'

GERALD SCARFE

Private Eye   April 30, 1965

Forget that bubble with words coming from LBJ's mouth; it is superfluous. What matters is the pose, the deliberate coarseness of it, Scarfe's intention to make a major statement. The details are lovingly eased into the figures; the bomb-shaped cufflinks; the obscene tongue of Wilson licking from the prison bars of his mouth; the saintly raising of LBJ's eyes, a sign that his mind is on higher things and those vast, flapping wings that make up his ears. Not a line is wrong, save perhaps for the unnecessary pistol hanging from LBJ's belt. Even those dots – coarse hairs or spots, they are sparingly used but acutely observed – on LBJ's bum add vital data to the sum of information. Of its kind – and this grotesque style has a long and noble tradition – this is a perfect cartoon. It scores a bull's eye on its target.

ABU

The Observer   June 13, 1965

Burning crosses had been observed on the top of a Midlands hill. There were blurred photographs in the press of men wearing the white sheets of the Klu Klux Klan in Britain. Later investigations showed the mainstay of the tiny band to be an old adherent of the lunatic fringe of the Far Right, a self-styled bodyguard to the leader of Britain's minute Nazi Party.

But how much was he the tip of a sullen iceberg of prejudice? The ease and speed with which the justification 'If black men move in round here the value of the house will fall' flashed round the country suggested that a white man's version of the bush telegraph was building. And in a general election, a Conservative candidate had won a safe Labour seat with a campaign that included the slogan 'If you want a nigger for a neighbour, vote Labour'.

'*You people lower the tone of the locality.*'

CUMMINGS

Sunday Express   July 9, 1967

This cartoon accompanied an article by Mr Enoch Powell, some ten months before his 'rivers of blood' speech dragged the question of immigration and racism firmly into the centre of the political arena. It cost Mr Powell his seat in the shadow cabinet, although he did not deviate one iota from previously-stated Conservative policy. It was the tone of his remarks that caused the fuss, the implication behind them that tolerant, liberal Britain could yet go through the violent agonies of the American Deep South. Powell's political career in the Tory Party was ended not because he is a racist, but because he cracked the shell of British complacency about our vaunted 'tolerance'.

But Cummings had been cracking the same shell, and ringing the same warning bell, for months before Powell. Had we not noticed, or did we need Powell's phrase 'rivers of blood', or Powell's vague story of a black man putting shit down a white old lady's letterbox, to cause the explosion?

EMMWOOD

Daily Mail   November 4, 1967

It sometimes seemed as if the unpopularity of the Wilson government, after its forced devaluation of the pound, its disastrous by-elections and its failure to deliver its promises of economic growth was relieved only by the pathetic and inadvertent clowning of George Brown. Thanks to him, the phrase 'tired and emotional' became a national euphemism for being drunk. But he was a sad jester, a failure in his economic plans, in his stint at the Foreign Office, and finally a failure in his political career.

Ten years on from that cartoon, and only Jim Callaghan and Peter Shore are still active in political life of the group around Wilson.

TROG

The Observer   October, 1969

When the fury of the new round of Irish troubles broke upon the British public in 1969, they could not begin to understand why people should be intense about different shades of religion. It took a lot of work by the Press to show that being a Catholic in Ulster's Protestant-dominated state was to be condemned to the worst housing, to the worst job opportunities and to a permanent second-class status.

Religious differences were another way of describing class divisions. The Protestant working class could at least claim to be better off than the despised Catholics, and so that great force of British reform, the Labour movement, was prevented by religious divisions from ever bringing Catholic and Protestant workers together for a common purpose.

The 'same God' covered a multitude of differences. The real trouble was that the Catholic minority (in Ulster) and the Protestant minority (in Ireland North and South) would only feel secure so long as they were part of different countries.

'It's just as well they believe in the same God.'

RICHARD INGRAMS

Private Eye June 21, 1968

The international student unrest of 1968, fuelled by Vietnam, by disillusion with the materialism of Western society and above all by the growth economy which had enabled the West to afford a mass student population, did very little damage and had little lasting political impact. The Paris stock exchange was burned, there was a general strike in France, riots and demos throughout the West, but in retrospect, the events were perhaps taken more seriously than they deserved. The 1968 student 'revolution' was as much the creation of the media which covered and promoted it, as that of the students.

Private Eye got it right, and got it funny, to poke fun at the serious occasion when the new student revolutionaries, Tariq Ali and Danny Cohn-Bendit, gathered to pay homage at Marx's grave.

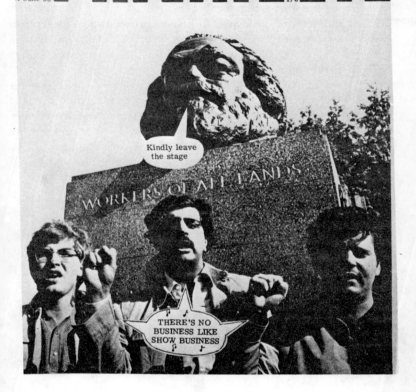

GARLAND

Daily Telegraph   January 19, 1970

Enoch Powell became anathema for the bulk of British Liberals for his doom-laden warnings about Britain's racial future. His arithmetic of immigration was often questioned, his motives for raising the issue were attacked and despised; he seemed to have ended his own political career by his obsession with immigration. But it became clear that his electoral influence was potentially enormous, and yet that he was not lending himself to the outlandish schemes of his supporters that he should launch a new movement, nor even that he was making any challenge for the Tory leadership. He seemed happy with his role as soothsayer, as the bearer of bad tidings. Slowly it became reasonable to wonder whether his motives had been honourable from the beginning. And when he again risked his political career to launch his campaign against the EEC, one wondered what sort of mad but honest prophet had infiltrated Britain's predictable political life; whatever he was, it was not evil.

'Where the seeds of the whirlwind have been sown, scarcely more than the first blades are yet above the surface.'

(ENOCH POWELL)

JAK

Evening Standard   January 14, 1971

It takes a combination of gall and supreme self-confidence to make a joke out of a bomb attack on a Cabinet Minister's home. JAK has both, although his only training for the job was working as a commercial artist for the *Evening Standard*. He has become one of the most popular, and sometimes one of the most controversial, of our cartoonists. Originals of his work hang in pubs and restaurants all over London; it is a city he moves around in, observing its style, capturing the flavour of the place and recording its fashions. His targets know when they are hit – when he portrayed the striking power workers as men with ever-grasping hands, thick skulls and holes where their hearts should be, he caused an industrial dispute on the *Standard*, as the printers threatened to strike in sympathy.

'It's the Residents' Association with a complaint about your wild party last night!'

IVOR

The Visor May, 1974

The Visor is the British soldier's own magazine in Northern Ireland. Produced by the troops themselves, it has a rare find in the soldier-cartoonist Ivor. He has the flavour of Belfast, the bombed and blasted shops, the rubble and litter, the devastated squalor which is the nearest any European city gets to the ghettoes of the US inner cities. The bulk of Belfast's depredation, by the way, is the fault not of bombs but of the BUM, the Belfast Urban Motorway.

Ivor's sense of detail is striking; you can tell the two characters are Provos – the UDA and UVF hard lads don't go for the flared trousers. They prefer their trousers fetchingly short in the leg, the better to show their elegant bovver boots. The mood that pervades Ivor's cartoons is one of hopelessness and professionalism. The Army will do its job, keep down the violence, but the squalor and the violence has bitten too deep into the city for a political solution to emerge. The Army, you feel, will be there as long as Belfast's squalor produces the thugs of the UDA and IRA.

'It's nice to be home – The conditions in the Kesh are disgusting Sean!'

LES GIBBARD

The Guardian *July 23, 1976*

Les Gibbard is a New Zealander, a devoted admirer of the work of Will Dyson, and one of *The Guardian*'s major assets. This cartoon makes a deep and fundamental and original point about the Micawberish way the British economy is 'run', and puts it squarely into a political context by presenting it as a fairy tale to mollify the Labour Left. It is a well-informed cartoon, foreshadowing the public spending cuts four months before they were announced. The final, felicitous touches are that atypical lullaby look on Denis Healey's face and, best of all, the speculators chuckling their way from the sleeping castle, portrayed as the wicked fairy.

'And so, the princess and entire kingdom fell into a deep sleep to await the day when the as yet unborn Prince Boom would come to awaken the princess with a kiss. . . .'

BRIAN McALLISTER

The Guardian   August 9, 1974

I have a soft spot for McAllister; I hired him for *The Guardian*. He brought in a cartoon of an old British couple standing on Beachy Head during one of the regular national crises of the 1970s. Charging up the cliff towards them came tanks, soldiers, aircraft, all emblazoned with swastikas and Iron Crosses. It was a full-scale invasion. The caption read: 'Looks like a last desperate attempt to restore the Dunkirk spirit.'

I hired him on the spot, for this remarkable gift of a dry wit, mixed with the imagination to bring together two entirely disparate events and make them fit and illuminate each other. This cartoon, just after Nixon's resignation, came at the time of calls for inquiry into the corrupt state of the North East Labour Party. It took McAllister to see how the two were made for each other.

'Your qualifications are perfect – it's just a matter of finding you a suitable constituency.'

JOHN KENT

The Guardian   March 22, 1976

Varoomshka is the Britannia of modern Britain, embodying the nation with a beautiful, poetic soul, ceaselessly harassed by its marauding politicians. Such, at least, is John Kent's cynical and often telling vision. But this is an entirely fair picture of the Wilson years, and the embarrassing praise that was heaped on him on his resignation as Prime Minister – just before the economic and political roof fell in with the IMF loan crisis of 1976 and the Parliamentary moves to chaos and coalition in 1977. Varoomshka's distraught reaction to Jim Callaghan was certainly premature and may prove to be unfair – although little in Callaghan's political career was impressive before he became Premier. He had been a dramatically unsuccessful Chancellor of the Exchequer, a determinedly unprogressive Home Secretary and a lame Foreign Secretary. Note Wilson's V-sign as he rises to the clouds, his banner meaning 'Without Principle', and the depth of plot and time Kent achieves through the strip-cartoon technique.

TROG

The Observer June 19, 1977

Harold Wilson was the first politician to note that national success in sports, or in achievements like conquering Mount Everest, somehow gave a boost to the popularity of the Government in power. British footballers had done little since their World Cup win in 1966, but in 1977 England had a formidable cricket side which won the Ashes from Australia. Whatever solace this gave to the British electorate was sorely needed. By-election defeats had worn down the Government's parliamentary majority; the trade unions had refused to consider a third year of wage restraint; industrial investment stubbornly refused to rise; street battles between the Police, the extreme Left groups and their bitter enemy, the National Front, had re-introduced political violence into British life. But the Government had managed to negotiate a pact with the Liberals, whereby their handful of votes in Parliament were pledged to Callaghan's Government – in exchange for some rather nebulous promises from the Prime Minister. The Liberal vote suffered in subsequent by-elections, but the threat of parliamentary chaos, and of yet another general election, was postponed. Trog's inspired cartoon catches the mellow flavour of a happy cricketing summer, the complacent bulk of Jim Callaghan, and shows David Steel, the young Liberal leader, protecting the Prime Minister's most tender regions.

JIM'S PROTECTOR

PHIL EVANS

Why you should be a Socialist   January, 1977

This was one of a number of cartoons which illustrated a lengthy pamphlet published by the Socialist Workers' Party, the largest of the British Trotskyist groups, as a recruiting effort. The cartoon makes a potent political point, leavened by the slapstick humour. It refers to the miners' strike of 1974, which led to the imposition of the three-day week for industry by the Conservative Government, in an attempt to save fuel. The solidarity of the miners themselves, and the support they won from the rest of the trade union movement, led the Heath Government to hold a general election on the issue of Who Rules Britain – Government or Unions. The Government lost; to the surprise of almost all the London-based political experts and pundits, who judged that thirty years of post-war prosperity had undermined working-class loyalties.

They had under-estimated the enormous boost to trade-union morale that had come from their defeat of both the Labour and Conservative Governments' legislative plans to make union-management agreements and contracts enforceable at law and they had under-estimated exceptional public sympathy for the miners. An attempt in 1972 to imprison five dockers under the Conservative legislation led to the threat of a general strike and their speedy release. The miners' strike of 1972 won similar support; police efforts to stop the miners' pickets from closing the Saltley coke depot were defeated when 30,000 men from the Birmingham engineering unions mobilized to back the miners.

A SELECT BIBLIOGRAPHY

British Cartoonists'
   Association
*Drawn and Quartered: The World of
the British Newspaper Cartoon
1920–1970*, London (1970)

Geipel, John
The Cartoon, London (1972)

Gombrich, E. H. and Kris, E.
Caricature, London (1940)

Klingender, F. D.
Hogarth and English Caricature,
New York (1944)

Low, David
Autobiography, London (1956)

Low, David
British Cartoonists, London (1942)

Lynx, J. J., (ed.)
The Pen is Mightier, London and
New York (1946)

Urquhart, Fred and
   Nicholson, Harold
WSC A Cartoon Biography,
London (1955)

Roth, Eugen
Simplicissimus, Hanover (1954)

Thomas, Graham (ed.)
Getting Them In Line, London
(1975)

Thomas, Graham (ed.)
Politics In Cartoon and Caricature,
in 20th Century Studies vols 13–14.
London (1975)

Jones, Michael Wynn
Cartoon History of Britain, London
(1971)

Cameron, James (ed.)
Vicky: A Memorial Volume,
London (1967)

Most of the cartoonists whose work appears regularly in the press have now published collections of their work. There are grievous gaps, most notably of Dyson's political work and the grand old men of *Punch*. But as early as 1902, even a provincial cartoonist like J. M. Staniforth of *The Western Mail* was publishing collections of his Boer War cartoons.

Historians will recognize my debt to A. J. P. Taylor's *English History 1914–45* (Oxford, 1965) and L. C. B. Seaman's *Post Victorian Britain* (London, 1966).

Most libraries can obtain bound volumes of *Punch*, which is the main source of cartoon research, but to probe deeper one must rely on the facilities of the British Museum's Newspaper Library at Colindale, to whose trustees and staff I am indebted.

INDEX

Abdication, the, 23, 126
Abu, 169; *Observer* cartoon of, 174
Abyssinia, invasion of, 120, 122
Adenauer, Konrad, 8
Affluent society, the, 166
America, see USA
Amin, Idi, 18
Andy Capp (comic strip), 21
Angel of Mons, the, 56
Angry Brigade, the, 24
Animal Farm, 25
Anne, Princess, 23
Anti-semitism, 15, 48, 125, 135, 136
Appeasement, 130
Arms race, 23, 48, 115
Ashes, the, 188
Asquith, H., 15, 43, 50, 62, 84, 86
Atom bomb, the: Illingworth's portrayal of, 19, 152; Low's perception of, 148; age of, 156
Attlee, Clement, 120, 134, 154
Australia, 12, 188
Austria, 55
Automation: threat of, 113, 161

Bairnsfather, Bruce, 11, 62; *Bystander* cartoons of, 78, 79
Baldwin, Stanley, 10, 97, 103, 105, 106, 114, 121, 126
Balfour, Arthur, 8, 31, 32
Balkans, the, 90
Ban the Bomb, 22
Battle of Britain, the, 138
Bayeux tapestry, the, 7,
Beaverbrook, Lord, 7, 11, 25, 106
Belfast, 182
Belgium, 54, 55
Berlin, 145, 147
Bevan, Nye, 155
Bevin, Ernie, 117, 120, 121
Birdsall, Timothy, 18; *Private Eye* cartoon of, 165
Bismarck, 150
Black Country, the, 50
Black market, the, 142
Blacks (negroes), 109
Blackshirt, The, 15; cartoon in, 125
Blackshirts, the, 116
Blitz, the, 17, 24, 64, 141, 145

Bloomsbury Set, the, 58
Boer War, the: comparison with Vietnam of, 22, 30; early reverses in, 28, 29; Stanniforth's portrayal of, 30
Bolsheviks, 100
Bolshevism, 12
Bomb, the, see atom bomb
Boxer (fictional character), 25
Boxer Rebellion, the, 30
Brer Rabbit (fictional character), 32
Breughel, Peter, 16
Bristow (*Evening Standard* comic strip), 17
Britain, 15, 20, 23, 24, 25, 36, 47, 48, 54, 60, 74, 82, 97, 118, 126, 128, 132, 134, 135, 143, 146, 147, 153, 156, 159, 165, 175, 180; cartoon symbols of, 8, 19, 29, 61, 102, 138, 151
Britannia: Tenniel's creation of, 8; Partridge's portrayal of, 68; Varoomshka as 186
British Army, the, 11, 20, 136; in the Boer War, 28; in Ireland, 42, 182
British Empire, the, 8, 21; in Boer War, 29, 30; Kaiser's threat to, 47; Strube's portrayal of, 103; casualty of the war, 150
British Legion delegation, 119
British Navy, the, 36, 67
British Trotskyist groups, 190
British Union of Fascists: magazine, 15; inception of, 110
Brown, George, 176
Bull, Joan, 17, 18
Bull, John: personification of Britain, 19, 30, 33, 54, 121; as Felix the Cat, 98; Baldwin as, 103
Butler, R. A., 160
Byestander, The: cartoons in, 62, 78, 79

Calais, 86
Callaghan, Jim, 19, 176, 186, 188
Carr, Robert, 24
Carroll, Lewis, 9, 120
Carruthers Gould, Francis, 7, 8, 12; *Westminster Gazette* cartoons of, 28, 31, 32, 33, 54, 86
Carson, E. H., 43
Carter, Jimmy, 20
Cartoonists: relationship with politicians of, 9–10; influence of, 10–11; distinctions between, 12; symbolic portrayal of countries by, 19; political hatred of, 22–3; American, 132; Nazi, 136; British, 144

POLITICS

AFRICA IN HISTORY Basil Davidson £1.50
A complete introduction to the history of the 'Dark Continent'.
Illustrated.

ANEURIN BEVAN Vols 1 & 2 Michael Foot £2.50 each
The classic political biography of post-war politics.

CRIME AND PERSONALITY H. J. Eysenck £1.25
A revised edition of the controversial and classic study of intelligence,
genes and aberration.

THE FEMALE EUNUCH Germaine Greer 75p
The book that caused a revolution, the central focus of the
Women's Liberation movement.

THE IMPERIAL ANIMAL Lionel Tiger and Robin Fox £1.00
The authors assert that humans are fundamentally undemocratic,
adulterous, acquisitive and status-seeking. A controversial
biogrammar of human behaviour by two brilliant anthropologists.

THE INTERNATIONAL URBAN CRISIS
Thomas L. Blair 60p
A lucid and disturbing analysis of the facts behind planning blight,
suburban sprawl, traffic congestion, and human alienation.

INTERVENTION AND REVOLUTION
Richard J. Barnet 75p
A biting critique of America's attempt at acting as world
policeman, guarding against the myth of the international conspiracy
of communism.

MARX'S GRUNDRISSE David McLellan 50p
A substantial set of extracts from the classic work in which Marx
develops an account of the process of alienation, analyses the nature
of work and develops a vision of the fully automated society in
which social wealth could be devoted to the all-round development
of the faculties of each individual. Edited by one of Britain's leading
Marxist scholars.

ARTS

ART AND THE INDUSTRIAL REVOLUTION
Francis D. Klingender £1.50
One of the most original and arresting accounts of the impact of
the new industry and technology upon the landscape of England
and the English mind. 'There is no book like it.' *John Betjeman.*
Illustrated.

FEAR   Les Daniels £2.50
A history of horror in the mass media from the earliest venal
dramas through gothic horror stories, Hollywood past and present,
illustration and rock music.

THE CITIZEN KANE BOOK
Pauline Kael, Orson Welles, Herman Mankiewicz £1.25
The complete shooting script and story behind one of the greatest
films ever made. Illustrated.

HITCHCOCK   François Truffaut £2.50
The classic interviews between two great film-makers now revised
and updated and available for the first time for some years.

FOLK SONG IN ENGLAND   A. L. Lloyd £1.50
The classic history of the natural expressions of the British people.

THE GREAT BRITISH PICTURE SHOW
George Perry £1.95
British cinema from the beginning.

MANKIND AND MOTHER EARTH
Arnold J. Toynbee £3.50
Arnold Toynbee's last book – a one-volume history of civilisation
that is breathtaking in its scope, scholarship and imagination.

MOVING INTO AQUARIUS   Sir Michael Tippett 75p
One of our greatest living composers asks: How does music, the
most expressive of all communication, relate to a technology-
obsessed society in which aggression and acquisitiveness have
become an index of personal worth?

ARTS

MYTHOLOGIES   Roland Barthes   75p
An entertaining and elating introduction to the science of
semiology – the study of the signs and signals through which
society expresses itself, from the leading intellectual star.

VILLAGES OF VISION   Gillian Darley   £2.50
Not every British village grew organically. Hundreds were built
by philanthropists, industrialists, landscape gardeners, or by half-
crazed visionaries. This is social history at its best – about
landscape, building and people.

THE VOICES OF SILENCE   André Malraux   £1.90
The ultimate exposition of all art from prehistory to modern
photography and cinema: the museum without walls.
600 illustrations.

FUNNY WAY TO BE A HERO   John Fisher   £1.50
An illustrated exploration of British comedians in the music hall
tradition, from Dan Leno, through Will Hay and Max Miller, to
Morecambe and Wise.

THE LONG VIEW   Basil Wright   £2.95
A complete history of the international cinema by a man who has
been involved in film-making for 50 years. Comprehensive,
massive, informative and entertaining.

A SONG FOR EVERY SEASON   Bob Copper   £1.25
A year in the life of a Sussex farming family . . . their work, their
traditions and above all their music and their songs.

SOCIOLOGY

THE WILD BOY OF AVEYRON   Harlan Lane   £1.95
The true story of a nine year old boy found living wild in the woods
outside Paris and of the attempts of a brilliant and enlightened
surgeon to 'civilise' him. The work of Itard was, and is, influential
in the education of deaf and dumb children.

PEOPLE TOGETHER   Clem Gorman   90p
A guide, handbook, and history of communal living in a 1970s
British context.

THE PROSTITUTION PAPERS   Kate Millett   50p
The prostitute is the archetypal exploited 'woman as object' – an
intense and arresting series of dialogues with New York prostitutes
by one of the leading figures in Women's Liberation.

BREAKDOWN   Stuart Sutherland   £1.25
One man's harrowing account of his own nervous collapse, the
treatment he received and its effects. This is followed by a full
evaluation of the merits and demerits of various kinds and systems
of therapy.

THE SOCIAL PHILOSPHERS   Robert Nisbet   £2.50
This provocative absorbing essay in social and intellectual history
shows that Western social philosophy has been preoccupied with
man's perennial quest for community: military, religious,
revolutionary, ecological and plural.

STEPS TO AN ECOLOGY OF MIND
Gregory Bateson   £2.50
This book develops a new way of thinking about the nature of
order and organisation in living systems, a unified body of theory
so encompassing and interdisciplinary that it illuminates all areas of
study of behaviour and biology.

SUBURBIA   David Thorns   60p
Is the suburb the successful fusion of town and country or a
mirror of the most depressing features of urban existence? A
critical analysis of the origin and components of suburbia.

WITHOUT MARX OR JESUS   Jean-François Revel   50p
The new American revolution has begun. It offers the only possible
escape for mankind today – the acceptance of technological
civilisation as a means and not an end.

SOCIOLOGY

THE CHILDREN OF THE DREAM Bruno Bettelheim £1.25
The dream is the kibbutz, one of the most enduring modern
attempts to create a Utopian human society. Bruno Bettelheim
examines the products of that dream and goes on to look at the
Western middle-class ideal of family.

CONSCIOUSNESS AND SOCIETY H. Stuart Hughes 75p
The re-orientation of European social thought from 1890 to 1930;
the ideas and works of Freud, Croce, Bergson, Jung, Sorel, Weber,
Durkheim, Proust, Mann, Gide, Hesse etc.

EDUCATION IN EVOLUTION John Hurt 60p
A classic of the history of education up to the Elementary
Education Act of 1870.

MODERN MYSTICS AND SAGES Anne Bancroft £1.95
Fourteen answers to one question. The greatest philosophical
minds of the Century précised – Gurdjieff, Aldous Huxley,
Teilhard de Chardin, Meher Baba, Martin Buber etc.

THE FEMALE EUNUCH Germaine Greer 75p
The book that caused a revolution, the central focus of the Women's
Liberation movement.

FOLK DEVILS AND MORAL PANICS Stan Cohen 50p
Teddy Boys, Mods and Rockers, Hell's Angels, football
hooligans, Skinheads, student militants, drugtakers: these are the
folk devils of our time. A classic study of deviancy sociology.
Illustrated.

HOMO HIERARCHICUS Louis Dumont 90p
Ostensibly a study of the caste system in India, Louis Dumont
sheds new light on Western notions of equality and democracy: a
classic of anthropology.

THE INTERNATIONAL URBAN CRISIS
Thomas L. Blair 60p
A lucid and disturbing analysis of the facts behind planning blight,
suburban sprawl, traffic congestion and human alienation.

TRAVEL

THE FEARFUL VOID   Geoffrey Moorhouse   £1.25
There is a fearful void out there in the empty quarter of the
Sahara Desert, but more terrifying still is the void within our
minds – the fear of loneliness and failure. One man's search to
conquer his own self-distrust. Illustrated in full colour.

JOURNEY THROUGH BRITAIN   John Hillaby   95p
It was a magical idea to walk through the over-industrialised land
of Britain from Land's End to John O'Groats, avoiding all centres
of population. Britain's master walker made his reputation with this
book. Illustrated.

JOURNEY THROUGH EUROPE   John Hillaby   £1.00
John Hillaby gives a splendid potpourri of factual account, lively
anecdote, mythology and private comment in this account of his
walk from the Hook of Holland via the Alps to Nice. Illustrated.

JOURNEY TO THE JADE SEA   John Hillaby   95p
Tired of city-living and ashamed of his toleration of boredom,
John Hillaby made a three-month safari from the Northern Frontier
District of Kenya to the legendary Jade Sea. Illustrated.

JOURNEY THROUGH LOVE   John Hillaby   £1.25
Hillaby's most recent and possibly most powerful and evocative
book concerns a series of several walks, in Yorkshire, Wales,
London, the South Downs and North America, and the thread
running through the narrative is the story of a great tragedy
and loss.